ARE WE GOING TO COMMIT SUICIDE?

*The Global Threat of Climate
Change and Nuclear War*

ALAIN F. CORCOS

Published by Wheatmark®
2030 East Speedway Boulevard, Suite 106
Tucson, Arizona 85719 USA
www.wheatmark.com

ISBN: 978-1-62787-771-8 (paperback)
ISBN: 978-1-62787-772-5 (ebook)

LCCN: 2019917059

Bulk ordering discounts are available through Wheatmark, Inc. For more information, email orders@wheatmark.com or call 1-888-934-0888.

rev202001

Through My Window

It is August 7, 2019. I am an old man looking through one of the windows of my house that overlooks my quiet neighborhood. Life has been mostly the same for the last 40 years, except that people come and go, kids are born, grow up, and leave. People act the same. They use their cars as much as they did before they heard about climate change. They talk about the price of gas but not about decreasing the use of vehicles that pollute the environment. They live in a state—Michigan—where the car is king. Few people take the bus.

Except for a few storms, Michigan has been fortunate not to deal with types of weather that affect Louisiana, Florida, Texas. We are lucky to not have to fight wildfires like in California. Thus, it is hard for us to believe that the world as we know it is changing, and worse, that it might disappear altogether.

I cannot blame people for continuing with their lives. After all, if they were thinking about climate change all the time, they would not be able to function. But, if we do nothing, we are doomed.

Contents

Preface

Beyond a certain point, the two great existential threats to our civilization, global warming and nuclear weapons, will lose their chains and join to rebel against their creators.

Nathaniel Rich

It is May 2019. Spring has finally come to Michigan. Nature is now smiling. Magnolia trees have finished blooming. Now it is tulip and cherry trees' turns, and then lilacs. Birds are singing. People are cleaning their gardens and starting to mow their lawns. Children are playing outside. However, there are clouds, not in the sky, but on the political horizon.

Once more nations menace each other with nuclear weapons, not realizing that if used, it will only take fifteen minutes to end the living world around due to thermal radiation. If we do not kill each other with nuclear weapons, climate change will bring about our death due to the pouring of carbon dioxide into the atmosphere. There were early warnings of such a catastrophe, but we did very little to prevent it. Today, seeing the real-time effects of climate change, most of us realize that we must stop the heating of the Earth.

We have taken the first steps towards this objective—turning to renewable energy.

However, the solution to this problem requires many sacrifices and changes in human behavior. The use of fossil fuels has given us a high level of civilization where engine power has replaced muscle power in every field including mowing the lawn and shoveling snow. But it is time to abandon this source of energy that is the primary reason for climate change and replace it by sources of energy that do not involve carbon dioxide or other greenhouse gases.

Let us hope that it is not too late for us to save our lives and those of our descendants.

Introduction

The abolition of war has become not only desirable but absolutely necessary if the planet is to be saved. It is an idea whose time has come.

Howard Zinn

In the last thirty years, we (the public) have become conscious that our climate has changed. We have seen more frequent serious heat causing drought, more rain and flooding, and vast fires in various parts of the world. The reason for climate change is not a secret. Scientists have told us that we are putting higher amounts of gases, such as carbon dioxide and methane in the sky. These gases allow some of the sun's warmth to escape into the atmosphere and reradiate back downward toward Earth's surface. With too much gas and too much heat the climate warms up, like what happens inside a greenhouse. The glass windows let the sun's rays in, but prevents others from getting out.

Solving climate change is very hard. Research by an array of scientists and scholars supports a daunting conclusion: Climate change is unlike any environmental problem we have ever faced. We can't fix it the way we started to fix smog or the ozone hole, with circumscribed regulations and treaties and limited technological changes. Climate change is too big in space, time, and complexity. The emissions that cause climate change are a central consequence of the some 7.5 billion people on Earth now, and within the next several decades some ten million will need to prosper on Earth.

Theoretically, the solution to the problem of climate warming is simple: decrease the quantity of greenhouse gases. But practically it is very difficult, because obviously, no nation can do it alone. There have been international meetings, but so far nothing concrete has emerged. And some nations do not want or cannot participate because of a lack of resources. We need an international government to enforce regulations, but today the political climate is not favorable for a rapprochement between nations.

There is no doubt that humans are responsible for the warming of our planet. It started when fire was invented. At that time, of course, our ancestors could not have imagined that one day their descendants would burn, coal, petroleum, and methane on a large scale. But today we know the severity of the warming of our planet (flood, droughts, hurricanes, etc.) and we must solve the problem as soon as possible unless we want to commit suicide.

We have not only affected the Earth's climate, but we have also polluted the air, especially in the big cities. Pollution kills a lot of people: It has been reported that pollution is responsible for the deaths of 1 million to 1.5 million Chinese annually. Pollution does not recognize borders. It is a global problem we have to solve together.

One cause of pollution is the large amount of exhaust emitted from cars, trucks, and planes. Worldwide petrochemical consumption has surged as hundreds of millions of people in China and other advancing countries can now afford airline tickets and fuel-guzzling trucks. This is one of the main reasons why we must turn to electric cars and bicycles.

Most people are aware that burning fuel in internal-combustion engines pollutes the air, but many are unaware that radioactive debris has also polluted our Earth, air, water. The oceans continue to be polluted with plastic debris, which fish mistake for food.[1] Lakes and rivers have been polluted with sewage, industrial waste, and the runoff from heavily fertilized farmlands (and lawns) resulting in fish disappearing. On the contrary, algae tend to flourish in this environment due to excess phosphate and nitrate. Pollution is a worldwide that should be solved internationally.[2]

During the long process of increasing our scientific knowledge and technical skills we have come into possession of enormous power, which we are using both constructively and destructively. Scientific advancements have taught us about the microscopic world (bacteria and viruses) thanks the electron microscope; the physical world of the atom thanks to the cyclotron; the cosmos thanks to the telescope; and recently we have even taken a picture of a black hole.[3] We are able to leave the Earth and explore other astronomical bodies (the moon so far, Mars next); we are on the verge of driverless cars that might prevent the millions of automo-

---

1   The problem with plastic is that it is not biodegradable, although the ocean waves and sunlight worm plastic into tiny bits. How long these bits remain in the ocean, we do not know, possibly 500 years or forever.

2   The French have come up with the idea to collect all the discarded plastic compounds and use them as road cover, that seems to last longer and is kinder to tires. Other countries should do the same.

3   True to science, the image is not of a black hole itself, which by definition cannot be seen in any wavelength, but of the so-called event horizon around it—the stars, dust and energy that circle the gravitational drain before being sucked inside for ever.

bile accidents each year; and we are working on a new quantum computer that will be far more powerful than anything around today. We have even started to understand how our brain works thanks to MRI scans. There seems to be no end in the progress of scientific knowledge and technology. Both work as partners.

For all our advancements, we are incapable of preventing wars and instead invent more powerful and sophisticated ways to kill each other. For thousands of years we killed each other by using rocks, clubs, swords, and guns. Now we have more efficient ways. Air planes were invented at the beginning of the 20th century and that led to the discovery that we do not need to be close to our enemies any more: we just bomb them from the sky. Recently, we have invented another method to kill our enemies from thousands of miles away using drones (self-driven planes that carry bombs, but no pilots).

War has become more and more uncontrolled and more deadly: from the poison gas used in World War I to napalm in Vietnam. Chemical warfare reappeared in the Iran-Iraq war of the early 1980s [4] and most recently in Syria. But the deadliest weapon remains the atomic bomb invented during World War II, which has led to the rise of nuclear weapons. In hopes of stopping the war, two atomic bombs were used to demolish the Japanese cites of Hiroshima and Nagasaki, which succeeded. The bombs were so powerful in killing

---

4   At one point in World War II, Winston Churchill ordered thousands of anthrax bombs from a plant that was secretly producing them in the United States. His chief advisor, Lord Cherwell, had told him that half a dozen bombers could carry enough four-pound anthrax bombs to kill very one within a square mile. However, production delays got in the way of this plan. See Howard Sinton's *War*. (New York: Seven stories Press), 155.

Japanese people that no nation has used one since. That is good, but what's bad is that countries continue to improve their atomic bombs knowing that if just one or two are used, the entire human race could be wiped out.

Yet, many people sincerely and earnestly believe that increasing our power to kill increases our security in some undefined way. It won't because we have reached the zenith of the art of killing. It should be obvious to anyone—but it is not—that warfare has become mutually destructive and suicidal. Yet, governments are unable to divert from the traditional international posture of threatening any enemy whether it be real or potential. Throughout history up to the present, most people believe that the welfare, prosperity, and power of the group into which they have been born into is more important than those of any other group. Along with that thought is also held: "Whenever we are frightened or feel threatened, the right, effective, and virtuous thing to do is to increase our ability to kill other people." That was the normal method of ensuring a group's survival in the past, but its success depended on the defensibility of the group or its ability to overcome competing groups.

It is time to realize that no nation—even the most powerful—can defend itself against other nations, nor can it effectively attack other groups, without great risk of complete destruction of its own people. In other words, it is no longer possible to "win" a war. Any war that involves atomic weapons between two nations, such as the U.S. and North Korea, will lead to the destruction of life on this planet.

Throughout history, if kings or emperors acquired some new weapons, sooner or later they were tempted to use it. Since 1945, however, humankind has learned to resist this temptation. By now we are accustomed to living in a world full of undropped bombs and unlaunched missiles: missiles

that are on display in parades in Moscow (Russia) or Pyan-
gang (North Korea) but are never fired. Let us hope that they
remain that way.

Public awareness of the terrible dangers of using nuclear
weapons might help the cause, but unfortunately, this seems
not to be the case. A recent study sought to examine how
important the topic of nuclear risk is to the American public: how much attention Americans give to it (if they thought
about it at all); and how they say they would respond if a
threat was imminent.

The results of the study were disappointing. In June 2018,
23 percent of Americans reported putting "no effort at all"
into thinking about the possibility of a nuclear attack and
how to prepare for it." And an additional 29 percent said
they put in "A little effort."

When asked to estimate the likelihood that they would
be affected by nuclear attack in their lifetime, Americans reported that on average, they thought it was slightly more
unlikely than likely, but just below the level of a "toss up."[5]
In other words, while Americans do not perceive a nuclear
detonation as impossible or highly unlikely, they reported
putting forth almost no effort to prepare for such an attack.
But, maybe these survey results are not astonishing because
there is no real possible preparation for an atomic attack: as
was the lesson in Hawaii when a false alarm was deployed
saying that a nuclear weapon was in route to the islands.

---

5   Kristin Karl and Ashley Lytle. This is not a drill: lessons from the
false Hawaiian missile alert. Htps://the bulletin.org/2019/01/this-is–
not-a–drill-lessons from-the false-Hawaiian-missile-alert.

Americans and the rest of the world should work to prevent such an attack.

It is time to make peace among ourselves not only because the next war might be the last one, but also because there are enormous dangers facing all of us. And those dangers do not know borders because they are human made. For hundreds of years, war shaped and reshaped the world's borders, moving the lines back and forth, causing states to grow and shrink. It created and destroyed empires. It generated new countries out of ashes. Everyone, including politicians and the public underestimate the dangers that face us. I suspect this is because they had never been taught the nature and capabilities of science and technology in high school or college.

Following World War II, many scientists who witnessed the horror brought on by one of their major scientific/military achievements (the atomic bomb) believed that the best way to avoid such catastrophic use of science in the future was to educate the public to the potential of employing science for evil well as for good, and to seek civilian control of nuclear energy. Thus, a loosely structured, but highly visible movement was born called "scientific literacy." Though, these attempts to educate the public have not been fruitful as explained in chapter 9.

A number of scientist organizations and public interest groups were formed in 1945, notably among these being the Federation of Scientists and the Federation of Atomic Scientists. Shortly afterward, in 1946, the Chicago chapter of the Federation of American Scientists began publishing the *Bulletin of Atomic Scientists* (later to become an independent journal and a highly regarded publication). The common element in all these activities was the belief that with the atomic bomb, science and technology had brought civilization to the edge of a precipice, and that lacking a more reasoned decision-making process regarding the use of such destructive technologies, civilization might well push itself over the edge.

Each year, the Bulletin of the Atomic Scientists sets a clock, called the Doomsday Clock, deciding whether the events of the previous year pushed humanity (and the rest of the living species) closer to or further from destruction. The closer to midnight we are, the more danger we are in. According to the clock, we are now two minutes from midnight.

In brief, we are faced with deadly dangers: pollution, climate change, and the use of nuclear weapons. To overcome them, we require the cooperation of all humanity. Shall we have it? [6]

---

6   Recently it seems that the public has become more aware of climate change than about the extinction of life on Earth by nuclear weapons.

1

Pollution

And man is now, whether he likes it or not, and indeed whether he knows or not (but it is important that he is beginning to know it), he is the sole agent for the future of the evolutionary process on this earth. He is responsible for the future of this planet.

Julian Huxley

Although I was born in Paris, I was raised on the French Riviera in a community called Roquebrune Cap Martin, next to the tourist town of Menton at the Franco- Italian border, located in a nice and very sheltered gulf. Its wonderful harbor and summer and winter festivals, especially the lemon one, call to tourists from all over the world. Before World War II, Menton was a quiet town of fifty thousand people, well known for its orange and lemon trees. The first foreign tourists to appreciate that part of France were the English. There is a statue in town of Queen Victoria who came to Menton to rest. Roquebrune is an old village and has a castle from the 9th century, which sits picturesquely on the side of the hill. The seaside of Roquebrune consists of the beach and a cape (Cap

Martin) with its old and beautiful pine trees.[7] In the bottom
of our hill was Winston Churchill's villa where he loved to
paint.

I came back to this beautiful part of the French Riviera
in 1978, when it still had its charm. According to my wife,
Joanne, I was very excited to again see where I was raised as
a young child. However, when I came back to France in 2006,
I did not recognize Menton. New hotels with underground
parking had been built and the traffic reminded me of San
Francisco or San Diego. The only building I recognized was
the Casino on the beach. The smell of orange and lemon trees
was replaced by the smell of exhaust from cars and buses.

Despite air pollution, tourists continue to visit, but cannot find a place to sit on the pebble beach. I was very disap-
pointed. But it was my fault: I had been warned by one of my
cousins in Paris that I should not have gone.

The next morning, I wanted to see the old village of
Roquebrune perched on a hill. And fortunately, it was as I
remembered it. The houses were beautifully painted and the
view of the sea was still spectacular. There was no air pollution there because cars have to be parked outside the village.
The Old Roquebrune is a village from the Middle Ages with
narrow streets and steps so that you can easily climb up and
down. I was pleased to see it again free of pollution as it was
years ago when I was a child. The name of my parents' villa
was Clair Matin (Clear Morning) for a good reason. It was so
clear one morning, years ago, that we could see the outline
of the Island of Corsica 140 kilometers away. Today, seeing
it from there would be impossible because of air pollution.

---

7   In the film Red Shoes, the lovers are in the horse-trained cab.
They do not know where they are. But I know. They were at Cape
Martin.

Pollution is the introduction of contaminants into the natural environment that causes adverse change. Major forms of pollution include air, light, plastic, thermal, visual, and water pollution along with soil contamination and radioactive contamination. In other words, we have managed to pollute everything around us.

Pollution started in prehistoric times when man created the first fire. According to a 1983 article in the journal *Science,* soot found on ceilings of prehistoric caves provides ample evidence of the high levels of pollution that was associated with inadequate ventilation of open fires.[8] But it was the industrial revolution that gave birth to environmental pollution as we know it today. London recorded one of the earliest extreme cases of water quality problems during the "Great Stink" of the Thames of 1858. Pollution issues escalated as population growth far exceeded the neighborhood's ability to handle their waste problems. Reformers began to demand sewer systems and clean water, which led to the construction of the London sewage system. In 1870, the same happened in Berlin, which was one of the worst cities in that respect in Europe.

The emergence of factories and consumption of immense quantities of coal gave rise to unprecedented air pollution. The factories' large volume of industrial chemical discharges added to the growing load of untreated of human waste. Chicago and Cincinnati were the first two American cities to enact laws ensuring cleaner air in 1881. Pollution became a major issue in the United States in the early twentieth century, as progressive reformers took issue with air pollution caused by coal burning, water pollution, bad sanitation, and

---

8   John D. Spengler and K.A. Sexton. "Indoor Air Pollution: A Public Health Perspective." *Science* 221 (4605) 9-17 (p9) 1983.

street pollution caused by the 3 million horses who worked in American cities in 1900, generating large quantities of urine and manure.

People saw the automobiles replacing the horses welcomed the cars as miracles of cleanliness. By the 1940s, however, automobile smog was a major issue in Los Angeles and still is in 2019. We are aware of the pollution cars cause, yet we continue to use them as individual means of transportation. My house is on a hill and I as I watch the cars and their drivers on the main street of East Lansing, Michigan, I notice most cars have only one occupant: the driver.

The problem of air pollution by internal-combustion engines is getting worse because worldwide petrochemical consumption has surged as hundreds of millions of people in China and other advanced developing countries have become able to afford cars, trucks, and airline tickets. According to a study published by in the Proceedings of the Academy of Sciences USA in March 2019, an estimated 102,000 people in the U.S. die from human-caused $PM_{2.5}$ pollution each year. $PM_{2.5}$ is named as such because the particles are 2.5 microns or less, generated by construction, fires, and the combustion of fossil fuels. These particles contain hundreds of different chemicals and can penetrate deep in the lungs, contributing to heart and lung disease.[9] These fine particles are a byproduct of our dependence on burning items like coal, gasoline, diesel, wood, trash, etc.

Recently I learned that traditional cooking methods that involve charcoal and kerosene also contribute to air pollution. Are we going to get rid of barbecues?

Air pollution cuts short the lives of far more people in

---

9   Douglas W. Dockery et al *The New England Journal of Medicine.* Vol 239, No24 (December 9, 1993).

the U.S.—estimates range from 107,500 to over 200,000 per year—than do traffic accidents. Together, indoor and outdoor air pollution cause one in every nine deaths globally in 2016—far more than the number felled by malnutrition, alcohol use, or malaria.[10]

We pollute not only the air, but also the streams, lakes, water supplies, and the oceans. We have polluted lakes and rivers with sewage, industrial waste, and runoff from heavily fertilized farmlands and lawns, fall out from nuclear explosions, chemical aerial sprays applied to crops, gardens, forests, and fields resulting in fish that are all but gone. However, algae flourishes due to excess phosphate and nitrate, both found in fertilizers. Many of the chemical agents in this alarming mélange imitate and augment the harmful effects of radiation. Among those are insecticides, pesticides and herbicides of every sort. Those of us who were born before 1940 cannot forget the history of the first organic insecticide, DDT, which was hailed for a while as a fantastic tool to stamp out insect-borne diseases. The problem with DDT was that it was not only killing the insects we did not want, but all the insects. Its harmfulness to humans was also unknown. One of its first uses was dusting thousands of soldiers, refugees, and prisoners during World War II to combat lice and mosquitoes.

In March 1944, after escaping Vichy France my brother, Gilles, and I enlisted in the French Air Force in Casablanca.[11] The French and the American soldiers were separated, but on the same airbase. The Americans used DDT and the French did not. I remember we had bed bugs, but not mosquitoes.

---

10   Tim Smedley, "Clearing the Air: The Beginning and the End of Air Pollution," *Bloomsbury Sigma*.
11   See my book, *The Little Yellow Train Escape from Vichy France*.

Obviously, there was enough DDT blowing from the American camp to the French camp. The fact that so many were in contact with DDT and did not suffer the ill effects of the chemical led people to believe it must be safe, though it is not. The misconception is understandable. DDT *in powder form,* is not readily absorbed through the skin. However, dissolved in oil, as it usually is, DDT is toxic. If swallowed, it is absorbed slowly through the digestive tract, and when breathed in, it may also be absorbed through the lungs. Once it has entered the body, it is stored largely in organs rich in fatty substances (because DDT is fat soluble) such as the adrenals, testes, or thyroid. Relatively large amounts are deposited in the liver, kidneys, and the fat of the large protective mesenteries that enfold the intestines,

My second encounter with DDT was when I came back from the war. I took over our family flower farm where we grew mostly carnations, a flower that requires a lot of care. They need to be sprayed with nicotine sulfate every few days with knapsack hand sprayers. I thought it was a terrible way to control bugs. It was then that I heard about DDT and discovered that I would only need to spray it every two weeks to control pests. At that time, I had no idea that I was also killing other kinds of insects and I was inhaling something that could kill me in the long run. Two years later I came to the U.S. to learn more about plant biology and never again got involved with DDT.

Is there another way to control insects rather than spraying insecticides? The answer is affirmative. One way is using a biological control, which consists of introducing natural enemies of insects that are troublesome to farmers. There are many examples of successful classical biological programs. One of the earliest successes was with the cottony cushion scale, a pest that was devastating the California citrus industry in the late 1800s. A predatory insect, the vedalia beetle, and a parasitoid fly were introduced from Australia. Within a few years the cottony cushion scale was completely controlled by these natural enemies. Although there are many successful biological control programs, there are few entomologists involved in these programs. Why should this be? The major chemical companies are pouring money into the universities to support research on insecticides. This creates attractive fellowships for graduate students and attractive staff positions. Biological-control studies, on the other hand, are never so endowed, simply because they do not promise anyone the fortunes made in the chemical Industry. These are left to state and federal agencies, where the salaries paid are far less.

Today water pollution is a big problem in cities around the world. Each year, water mains and pipes leak an estimated 20 percent of their water.[12] The result is not only underground damage to city streets and wasted water, but that wasted water becomes polluted, picking up all kinds of junk in its path. Stopping even half of those leaks could provide water to meet the daily needs of hundreds of millions of people. Hope is under way. Mini robots are now inserted into fire hydrants to swim through water mains of all sizes to find leaks. These robots then share the precise locations of damaged pipes.

In 1935, when I was just 10 years old, I saw my first plastic object: a cup. Since then, we have polluted the oceans with our plastic waste. We can see—bottles, bags, discarded fishing nets, and all manner of other objects, littering shorelines and bobbing in oceans. According to a U.N. biodiversity report, published May 6, 2019, pollution from plastics has gone

---

12   *Nature Conservancy Michigan Summer 2019*, page 37.

up tenfold since 1980. And there's the plastic waste we can't see: micro plastics, whittled by the sun, wind, and waves into bits so small that some are visible only under a microscope. Scientists are just beginning to understand the impact these particles have on fish (that mistake plastic for food) the food chain, and ultimately us. [13] The amount of plastic waste is incredible. It has been estimated that 1.15 million to 2.41 million tons of plastic waste enter the ocean each year from rivers.[14] Plastic garbage accumulates in five different patches in the world's oceans. The largest in the Pacific lies between Hawaii and California and covers an estimated surface area of 1.6 million square kilometers, twice the size of Texas or three times the size of France. This is a global problem.[15] A small positive step has been taken when it was found that bacteria can be engineered to consume corn sugar and produce polyester that can be used to make biodegradable plastics, including the types used in shopping bags.[16]

There is a lack of awareness when it comes to radioactive debris. The development of nuclear science introduced radioactive contamination, which can remain radioactive for hundreds of thousand years. Lake Karachay—named

---

13   And so do whales. On March 16, 2019, a dead whale washed up in the Philippines with 88 pounds of plastic in its stomach. *Time* April 1, 2019, p 4.

14   More than 600,00 tons of plastic microfibers are estimated to enter the ocean each year, shed from fleece, Polyester, and other synthetic fabrics during washing. *National Geographic*, March 2019, p 26.

15   Recently two young officers of the French Merchant Marine created a special boat capable of recycling plastic or use it as a fuel. On the other hand, American scientists have discovered that some marine organisms destroy plastics for their own benefit. See *Sciences et Avenir*, November 2017.

16   Peter Faitley. A plastic goes commercial. *Technology Review.* July August 2007, p 14.

by the Worldwatch Institute as "the most polluted spot on earth" served as a radioactive debris disposal site for the Soviet Union throughout the 1950s and 1960s. Despite nuclear weapons' deadly effects on life in general, nuclear weapons continued to be tested, often multiple times while in development.

The Earth is not the only place polluted. Earth's space is becoming increasingly littered with debris. A satellite could be demolished if struck by a softball- sized piece of junk. Even a one-centimeter tidbit could disable a spacecraft. The collision problem has become so serious that in 2016 the European Space Agency which tracks the objects, announced it might capture derelict satellites in low orbits starting in 2023. Clutter is arising fast as more countries and companies launched electronics. Again, pollution is a global problem that we need to solve together.

Although we are aware of the dangers of pollution and we are combating it by many means, the future is not bright because of Earth's ever-increasing population. There were three billion people on Earth in 1965; [17] today the number is 7.6 billion and counting. [18]

Pollution is a killer. In one of the most extensive reports of its kind, environmental health experts estimated that nine million premature deaths worldwide —16% of all deaths— were linked to pollution in 2015, with most deaths resulting from air pollution.[19] According to the World Heath Organization, more than 1 million people in China died from the

---

17   Larry K.Y. Ng. and Stuart Mudd co-editors *The Population Crisis* (Bloomington: Indiana University Press, 1965). 5.

18   Roy Scranton. *We Are Doomed. Now What?* (New York: Soho Press, 2018), 322.

19   *The Lancet.* Vol. 390, October 19, 2017.

effects of ambient air pollution in 2016.[20] Deaths from pollution-linked diseases, like heart disease and cancer, were three times higher than deaths from AIDS, tuberculosis, and malaria combined. Ninety-two percent of pollution-related deaths happen in low and middle-income countries like India, China, Pakistan, Bangladesh, Madagascar, and Kenya. In 2015, pollution was linked to 1.8 million deaths. In India, it was linked to 2.5 million deaths. In the United States, despite legislation and regulation of cleaner air and water, pollution is also killing people. More than 155,000 deaths in 2015 were related to pollution.

Pollution is a very serious problem that can affect everyone, but not everybody at the same time. Humanity can survive; but climate warming—the topic of the next chapter—affects everyone at the same time and is a problem that must be solved globally or we will not survive.

---

20   Rachel Hartigan, May–June. *National Geographic,* June 2019, 28.

2

Climate Change

*The specter of global warning unites humanity in a common
task. Every time anyone in the world lights a wood stove or
starts a car, or burns an acre of forest, the atmosphere receives
another dose of carbon dioxide and other greenhouse gases
that threaten catastrophes in decades or centuries to come.*

Jose G. Goldemberg[21]

Despite killing each other, wars, famines, and diseases, our
species has been very successful on Earth. There are billions
of us. But with success we have warmed the planet's climate
to the point that we may not survive unless we unite to solve
this global problem.

As the planet warms, look for more rain,[22] flooding where
it is already wet, and deeper drought where water is already
scarce; look for more deadly and frequent hurricanes and

---

21   This epigraph was written by Jose Goldemberg. Brazil's secretary of state for science and technology, in his book *How to Stop
Global Warning*. 1990.
22   This is not a surprise to scientists. Warner air holds more mois-
ture, which creates the potential for bigger storms.

wildfires; look for drying lakes; look for ice to thaw and sea levels to rise.[23]

It might hurt our pride, but it is important to know that we responsible for climate change. The effect was very small when fire was invented, but today, all seven billons of us are responsible for putting large amounts of carbon dioxide and other gases into the atmosphere, resulting in climate change. (See next chapter: the greenhouse effect.)

The shifts of climate change are already here and have shown to be catastrophic. These shifts include rising sea levels, stronger tropical cyclones, more intense precipitation and flooding, more frequent droughts and wild fires, the melting of glaciers and the changing seasonality of snowmelt. For example, when a river dries up, a whole way of life comes to an end. This is happening in South Eastern Australia where the marginally fertile lands of the Murray-Darling region were transformed into the breadbasket of Australia through a massive water-management program that dammed rivers, filled reservoirs, and tapped water for irrigation and other human needs. But today, after seven years of drought and decades of warmer temperatures, farmers have been brought to their knees.[24] This nearly happened in California after years of drought, but fortunately it finally rained and snowed in 2017, 2018, and 2019.

Climate change affects all parts of the word. Longyearbyen, Norway, is the northern most town in the world, but its 2,000 inhabitants wish it would be colder. Because melting permafrost and higher temperatures have caused havoc in re-

---

23   Global average sea level has risen by about 7-8 inches since 1900, with almost half (about 3 inches) of that rise occurring since 1993. *USA Today*, November 4, 2007.

24   Robert Draper. Australia Dry Run. *National Geographic Magazine* April 2009, p 35.

cent years, triggering deadly avalanches on the steep mountains that flank the town. Houses have been destroyed, and some areas have been closed or declared unsafe. Hundreds of residents have been affected; some have had to evacuate their homes because the melting permafrost created dangerous cracks in the foundation of their homes.[25]

Glaciers are melting. Seas are rising; we already know how ocean water will move inland along the Eastern Board, the Gulf of Mexico and other coastlines around the world. What scientists are urgently trying to figure out is whether the inundation will be much worse than anticipated—many feet or a few. The big question is, "are we entering an era of even faster ice melt?" The answer depends greatly on how the gigantic Thwaites Glacier in west Antarctica responds to human decisions.[26] As the ice sheets on Greenland and Antarctica shrink in the next few centuries, seas could rise 20 feet,[27] destroying many big cities, including Miami[28] and New York. Most mountain glaciers are thinning.[29] The consequence is that there is less melting in the spring and droughts will be intense as they were in the early 2010s in California. In Asia where glaciers feed the greatest rivers, lifelines for at least two billion people are at risk.[30] It is not surprising that a warming climate is melting the world's glaciers and

---

25   *USA Today*. Sunday, December 10, 2017.
26   Richard B. Alley. "Is Antarctica collapsing?" *Scientific American*, February 2019, p 40.
27   Tim Appenzeller. "The Big Thaw," *National Geographic*, June 2007, p 58.
28   Laura Parker. "Treading Water," *National Geographic Magazine* February 2015, p 207.
29   "The Big Thaw." See footnote 13. These articles in *National Geographic Magazine* are very informative with their pictures and maps of the future.
30   "The Big Melt." *National Geographic*. April 2010, p 67.

polar ice, but no one expected it to happen this fast. Greenland's ice sheet once seemed too big to melt substantially. Now as weather warms, the ice is disintegrating faster. Scientists think that this could continue for centuries and eventually change the island's geography and the planet's sea level. Greenland's melting ice alone could push the sea level up approximately ten feet over the next century, if greenhouse effect doesn't let up.[31]

Among the icy regions that now thaws far more than it used to is the Artic.[32] As polar ice retreats, the Northwest Passage could become an economically viable sea route. But consequences for pristine Artic regions could be devastating. Increased shipping traffic could lead to more carbon deposits on ice and snow, and higher risks of fuel leakage or spills. The world's oceans are warming at a rate faster than previously estimated per a study in *Science* released in early January 2019. Melting Artic ice pours an estimated 14,000 tons of water into the Earth's oceans every second, making it the biggest contributor to rising sea levels.

The first nations to disappear will be the island nations of the Pacific. King tides already inundate villages with knee-high waters. When this happens the villages are abandoned and the locals are relocated. The leaders of these island nations have a goal: make the world respond to the urgency of climate change.[33]

Climate change not only affects our lives, but also the lives animal and plant species. They must adapt or perish. In the past it would take millions of years for temperatures

---

31   Tim Appenzeller. "The Big Thaw," *National Geographic,* June 2007, p 56.

32   Andy Isaacson. "Into Thin Ice," *National Geographic Magazine,* January 2016, p 106.

33   Justin Worldland. "Sinking," *Time,* June 24, 2019, p 32.

to change drastically, but today it happens within decades. Nothing that we know about evolution suggests that plants and animals can rapidly adapt to such a change, meaning massive extinctions should be expected.[34]

Plants may survive climate change better than animals, but it is doubtful that they would survive what Jonathan Schell and others call the nuclear holocaust.

Scientists have studied irradiation of plants and discovered that a gamma-ray dose of ten thousand rads[35] would be enough to devastate most vegetation, and that large plants are more vulnerable to radiation than small ones. Trees are among the first to die, grasses among the last. The most sensitive trees are pines and the other conifers, for which lethal doses are in roughly the same range as those for mammals (two thousand rads).

According to a U.N. biodiversity report (May 6, 2019) explained that the loss of species is now happening "tens to hundreds of times" as fast as the average rate over the past 10 million years, which poses a dire threat to ecosystems all over the world. The loss of biodiversity is not just a problem for nature lovers. Human life is inextricably linked with natural ecosystems, because three-quarters of crops depend on insect pollination. Some $777 billion worth of crops could be lost each year if pollinators were to die out.[36]

Furthermore, the warming is changing what animals eat,

---

34   Mark Fihetti. "Rising Temperatures Hit Species Hot Spots," *Scientific American*, August 2014, p 84.
35   The rad is a unit of absorbed radiation dose defined a rad=0.01 Gy=0.01 J/kg. It was originally defined in CGS units in 1953 as the dose causing 100 ergs of energy to be absorbed by one gram of matter. The material absorbing the radiation can be human tissue or silicon microchips of any other medium for example, air water, lead shielding, etc.
36   UN biodiversity Report, May 6, 2019.

where they rest, and how they raise their young.[37] On the other hand, plant species may begin to spread. For example, the Antarctic has warmed so much so that tufts of the continent's few native plants as well as some invasive species, are spreading.[38]

Climate change also negatively affects the oceans. The increase in carbon dioxide in the atmosphere is in turn making the ocean more acidic. This thought is setting off alarms in the minds of marine biologists, because a more acidic ocean means that coral may not be able to get enough calcium from seawater, which is needed to build their protective calcium-carbonate shells.

When I was a child in the 1930s, I learned to ski in the Swiss Alps and at that time there was never a problem with a lack of snow. In fact, there was sometimes too much of it. But today, due to climate change, the Alpine snow season has been shortened by 38 days. It starts 12 days later and ends 26 days earlier than before 1960. Europe experienced its warmest-ever winter in the 2015-16 season, with snow cover in the Southern French Alps at just 20 percent of its typical depth. December 2016 was the driest in 150 years of record keeping, and the flakes that did manage to fall did not stay around long. The snow line—the point on a slope at which it's high enough and thus cold enough for snow to stick—is about 3,900 ft.—a historic high in some areas. But worse lies ahead as scientists predict the snow line will be at 10,000 ft. by the end of the century.

The resort town of Aspen, Colorado, kicked off its own climate-change study more than ten years ago. The city leaders sought the advice of leading scientists in climate

---

37   "A Crack in the World," *National Geographic*, March 2019, p 115.
38   Ibid. p 135.

change and devoted $145,000 to a pair of local studies. The announcement of the studies' findings a year later bore the somber headline, "Aspen Climate Study Finds Serious Risk to the Future of Skiing." At first blush, the emphasis on skiing may provoke eye rolling. But as Aspen goes, so goes any other mountain area. Aspen leaders have to come to grips with the fact that by the end of the century there may be too little snow not only for skiing but for replenishing water supplies, sustaining fishing, and fighting fires, which would be more frequent in water-starved forests. Aspen may need to put ski lifts higher up the mountain and, eventually, plan for life after skiing.

Rising temperatures during the 20th century have caused the ice to melt in Greenland. Researchers say 7,500 gigatons of ice—equal to the weight of more than 20 million Empire State Buildings—have melted into the ocean over that time.

Climate change deniers must be blind to not see that the storms in the last few years have been the worst on record. In 2017, storms slammed the East Coast, Gulf Coast, and the Caribbean. Violent winds and floods led to the deaths of thousands of people, caused hundreds of billions of dollars in damage. They devastated untold acres of wildlife habitat, from coral reefs to inland forests. Mostly to blame, is a trio of record breaking back to back hurricanes. In August, the hurricane Harvey doused parts of Texas with more than four feet of rain, flooding a third of Houston and all 22 of the city's bayous. In September, hurricane Irma savaged Barbuda with sustained winds of 185 miles per hour and then roared into Florida, becoming the state's costlier hurricane at upwards of $50 billion in damages. Maria followed, ruthlessly whipping the islands of Hispaniola and Puerto Rico with winds of 155 miles per hour, stripping forests, crippling infrastructure and leaving homes and lives in ruins. [39]

In September 2018 Hurricane Florence devastated North Carolina. The true danger was not the wind it brought, but the water. Over 2 feet of rain fell in parts of North Carolina, which broke state records. Flooding in Wilmington transformed the coastal city into an island, preventing people and supplies from getting in and out. A 10-foot storm surge flooded the city of New Bern. Two years before North Carolina was deluged by Hurricane Mathew, which was said to be a 500 years flood. But Hurricane Florence became a two-year flood. It is not too early to know what 2019 will bring—I am writing this in June 2019—it already looks like the worst year yet for floods.[40]

Florida's famed wetlands, the Everglades, are pinched between a burgeoning Miami to the east and encroaching saltwater to the west. With sea levels rising, the immense freshwater marsh hangs in the balance. By 2100 most of this unique treasure could be dramatically altered.

The link between climate change and wildfires is fairly straightforward. Warmer temperatures transform the fire season into a year-round phenomenon while dry weather kills off vegetation, creating fast-burning tinder, especially in California, which has become warmer and drier. The Golden State, like the rest of the planet, has experienced continuous

---

39   According to a study by the National Oceanic and Atmospheric Administration, that hurricane season was fueled in part by unusually warm ocean water, and it is predicted we will see more active hurricane seasons like 2017 in the future. *USA Today,* 9.29, 2018,
40   The most recent hurricane was the hurricane Dorian that tore through the Bahamas as a category 5 at the end of Labor Day weekend 2019 destroying and flooding everything in its pass. It hit also the eastern coast of the U.S. but with less force.

record or nearly record-breaking temperatures over the past decade. On top of that, the state suffered a historic drought that lasted more than five years and killed millions of trees. This combination has contributed to the destruction of houses and lives caused by wild fires.[41] The town of Paradise, California was completely destroyed in 2018 and is a recent deadly example.

At the opening of the United Nations climate change conference in Poland in December 2018 Secretary-General Antonio Gutters made a short speech with a long history. The twenty warmest years on record, he said, have occurred in the past twenty-two years with the last four years being the four warmest; the concentration of carbon dioxide in the atmosphere is the highest it has been in three million years.[42]

About twelve years ago Jeffrey Sachs wrote that "induced climate and hydrological change is likely to make parts of the world uninhabitable, or at least uneconomic. Over the course of a few decades, if not sooner, hundreds of millions may be compelled to relocate because of environmental pressures."[43] My question is, where will people relocate? Regions farther inland than the coastal areas are also affected by climate change. Hundreds of millions of people, including the poorest farm households, live in river valleys where irrigation is fed by melting glaciers and snow. The annual snow melt is earlier every year, synchronizing less with the summer grow-

---

41   With nine of the state's 20 most destructive fires blazing since 2015.

42   In order to know that, generations of scientists have analyzed the content of tiny pockets trapped in ancient Antarctic ice and counted the number of microscopic stomata—portals of the intake of carbon dioxide-on the surface of fossilized leaves.

43   Jeffrey D. Sachs. "Climate Change Refugees," *Scientific American*, June 2007, p 43.

ing season and glaciers are disappearing altogether. Lack of water or too much at a time will affect everyone no matter where you are.

Climate change presents one of greatest tests humans have yet faced. New technologies and new habits offer some promise, but only if we move quickly and decisively, which is not forthcoming. What explains the lack of decisive progress on human-driven climate change? Very likely a lack of funding for research, industry influence on politics, poor media coverage, and doubt-sowing by those invested in fossil fuels, an opposition to government intervention, and a lack of imagination. It is time for scientists and leaders of every nation to join forces and solve climate change or we will all die.

Altering the course of climate change is a task that will take decades. It will require innovative new technologies and overhauls of the world's energy, agriculture, and transportation. It is toward these objectives that federal money should be invested, not in building manufacturing facilities like Solyndra, which ended in bankruptcy. These companies had interesting technologies, but none was ready for the challenge of building commercial products and selling them in highly competitive markets. We need to create cleaner ways to produce energy. This will require new knowledge in physics and chemistry and lead to advanced technologies that can compete in cost with fossil fuels. We might be able to do this, if we go to work immediately.

I had a neighbor, the late Albert Newman, who thought we should transfer water from flooded regions to the dry ones. Today, Newman's idea does not seem so crazy. Every time there is a flood there is loss of life and a lot of suffering. Newman's idea would require a lot of money, but more is being lost each time a flood occurs. As to the engineering of such a vast program, perhaps it can be accomplished with the construction of artificial lakes and large pumping stations. It would be a challenge, but it may not be impossible.

There are no borders to climate change: the sea does not recognize them, nor do the earthquakes or hurricanes, which might hit Puerto Rico, Japan, Haiti, or India. These storms have resulted in terrible destruction in lives, homes, and buildings and create future problems that must be solved internationally.

Take Hurricane Katrina, the costliest natural disaster in the United States

History,[44] which hit New Orleans and coastal Mississippi, where twenty-five feet of water split entire buildings and killed hundreds of people.[45] New Orleans is in one of the lowest spots in the United States—as much as 17 feet below sea level in some areas—and it continues to sink by up to an inch a year. Upstream dams and levees built to tame the Mississippi River floods and ease shipping have starved the delta downstream of sediments and nutrients, causing wetlands that once buffered the city against storm-driven seas to sink beneath the waves. Louisiana has lost 1,900 square miles of coastal lands since the 1930s; Hurricanes Katrina and Rita took out 217 square miles, putting the city that much closer to the open Gulf. Sea levels could rise several feet over the next century and flood the whole region. Are we going to move New Orleans inland and break the levees so the Mississippi can start to put sediments back into the delta?

Very recently I heard that some politicians are thinking it

---

44   We do not know how much the 2017 hurricane Maria that hit Puerto Rico will cost.

45   Rick Luettich. Mississippi and Alabama are close to ideal for maximum storm surge. *National Geographic Magazine*, p 71.

might be more economical and reasonable to move cities to higher ground away from rivers and oceans, than to rebuild on the same spot. Could this be possible?

Although climate scientists know that unchecked, man-made global warning will wreak havoc on the planet and many polls show that Americans understand that climate change is happening, people choose to do nothing about it. On October 8, 2018, a landmark a U.N. report rings what scientists hope is a forceful enough alarm to wake the world up.[46] They warned us that a global temperature rise of 1.5 degrees C. is a threshold the planet cannot cross without seeing some of the worst effects of climate change. According to them, this could happen as early as 2030 if greenhouse gases continue to be released at the current rate. [47]

In the last few years, the effects of climate change have been so obvious that people are now conscious of the fact that we need to solve this global problem quickly. The solution will not be easy. We can get electricity from renewable energy (wind, solar), but the growth in renewable energy has made virtually no dent in the use of fossil fuels. It has come largely at the expense of nuclear energy, another low-carbon source. But, under the shadow of the Fukushima tragedy a nuclear comeback looks increasingly unlikely. Theoretically, nuclear energy is the best technologically, but it requires perfect engineering, location, and control.

Can we adapt to climate change? It is going to be difficult because the change is so fast. Take the example of crops. We need varieties engineered for resilience as the region becomes hotter. But creations of new varieties take time even

---

46   Justin Worland. "Climate Catastrophe Seen Just 12 Years Away," *Time*, October 22, p 12.

47   See the next chapter in which I explain the greenhouse effects.

with the new tools of transferring genes from one organism to another. The right genes need to be found, but there is no guarantee that they exist. It has been suggested that humans might start to get accustomed to eating other types of food. This could be hard for Americans who generally refuse to eat meats frequently eaten by Europeans, such as rabbit, lamb, and horse meat.

More than fifty years ago, when I was working on my PhD in plant breeding, I asked my major professor why no one in the department was thinking of transforming algae into food. He had no answer. Today, in Mexico, where seaweed blooms caused by warming sees threatening to strangle the tourist industry, researchers are working to turn the invasive species into food or fuel.

Obviously, it is time for us to realize that climate change is real and that we have to stop the emission of greenhouse gasses in the air. However, cutting greenhouse gas emissions is not enough to stop global warming. At this point, we must remove some of the carbon dioxide that is already in the atmosphere. The good news is that there are plenty of solutions for that. The bad news is that those methods generally require huge amounts of energy and good will. The history of attempts to control the greenhouse effect have been lamentable so far. Too few people understand that we are all responsible for climate change. Instead of blaming each other we need to cooperate and lessen the damage that we have done to our home.

In brief, if we want to save humanity from the danger of climate change due to the warming of the Earth, by 2050 we need to: decline our use of natural gas by 62 percent; get rid of coal; use renewable energy like wind and solar to make 97 percent of total electricity; develop better technologies; use nuclear power; invent ways to remove carbon from the atmosphere; and increase the acreage of our global forest instead of destroying it (changing what we eat so less land is needed for agriculture). Such a program requires tremendous will and sacrifices from us.

3

The Greenhouse Effect

No one knows when the debate on global warming will be resolved by scientists, but it is one with which every citizen should be familiar. How we got from Jean-Baptiste-Joseph Fourier two centuries ago to our current predicament makes for a fascinating albeit deeply tale –and I hope, for interesting reading as well.

Gale E. Christianson

In the previous chapter I mentioned the term, "greenhouse effect" a few times. It is important because it is responsible for the noticeable climate change that seriously affects the whole world. What is the greenhouse effect? One day in the early 1820s, Jean-Baptiste Fourier, the French savant, began to ponder the question of how Earth stays warm enough to support the diverse range of flora and fauna inhabiting its surface. Why is the heat generated by the sun's rays not lost after striking and bouncing off the great oceans and landmasses of the world? Taking pen in hand, he wrote down a novel hypothesis. Much of the heat does in fact escape back into the void, but not all. The invisible dome that is the atmosphere absorbs some of the sun's warmth and reradiates it back downward to Earth's surface. Fourier likened this thermal envelope to a domed container made of glass, a gigantic bell jar formed out of clouds and invisible gases. In coming together, the water vapor and other gases simulate a vault that receives and conserves heat, without which all life would surely perish. Fourier was ahead of his time. His explanation of how the Earth stays warm led to the explanation of today's climate change. He should be recognized as the father of the greenhouse effect.

Scientists have known for quite a while that the Earth has been warming. For example, in 1989 environmentalist Jessica Tuchman Mathews was interviewed by Bill Moyers in which she said about the greenhouse effect:

> It is a natural phenomenon. If we didn't have the greenhouse effect, this would be a lifeless, ice-covered planet. What is new is that through combustion of fossil fuels and the deforestation of tropical forests, we are accelerating this phenomenon so fast that it's throwing the system out of equilibrium. You see radiation comes from the sun, passes through the atmosphere, and hits the earth. Some of it is absorbed by the earth, and some of it is re radiated back to the atmosphere. These so-called greenhouse gases that we're emitting absorb that radiation to our atmosphere and it heats it up. One of the gases is carbon dioxide. Until a few years ago, we thought carbon dioxide was the whole problem. Then, we discovered a number of others: the chlorofluorocarbons, the CFC's, which are also the gases that are depleting the ozone layer in the stratosphere, methane, which is a natural gas, nitrous oxide which also comes from

combustion; and ozone here in the low atmosphere. And those are just the principal ones.[48]

Today extreme temperatures, erratic rainfall, floods, drought, tropical cyclones, rising sea levels, tidal surges, salinity intrusion, and ocean acidification are causing serious negative impacts not only on the lives and livelihoods of millions of people around the world, but also on animal and plant species. No credible climate scientist doubts that humans have influenced Earth's climate during the last two centuries, primarily by causing increases in the concentrations of greenhouse gases,[49] such as carbon dioxide and methane, in the atmosphere. These gases trap radiation emitted from Earth's surface after it has been heated by the sun and the added heat is retained in Earth's atmospheric envelope, making its climate warmer. They are called greenhouse gases because the same phenomenon happens in a greenhouse. The glass tends to pass visible light but absorb infrared rays. In other words, the infrared energy remains trapped inside the greenhouse because it cannot pass out again through the glass. Carbon dioxide makes a huge greenhouse of the Earth, allowing the sunlight to reach the Earth's surface but limiting radiation of the resulting heat into space.

Such a fact took years for scientists to believe, but in 1988, Jim Hansen told a group of reporters in a hearing room, just after testifying to a Senate committee, "It is time to stop waffling so much and say that the greenhouse effect is here and it

---

48 Bill Moyers. *A World of Ideas* (London: Doubleday, 1989), 292.
49 Gases in the atmosphere such as carbon dioxide do what the roof of a greenhouse does. During the day, the sun shines and the earth warms up, but the heat does not escape like it should during the night. This is what we call the greenhouse effect that keeps some of the sun's energy from escaping back into space at night.

is affecting our climate now.[50] In December 2006 Hansen gave a talk in honor of greenhouse pioneer Charles David Keeling who monitored carbon dioxide on the summit of Hawaii's Mauna Loa for almost 50 years, from 1958 until his death. Keeling demonstrated that the concentration of atmospheric carbon dioxide had been rising the whole time.[51] During his talk Hansen showed his audience the most striking climatic graph of the relationship between atmospheric carbon dioxide, average Earth temperature, and sea level during the last 400,000 years. The amount of atmospheric carbon dioxide has increased 32 percent since 1850. Any reasonable person can conclude that the Earth is getting warmer and humans are causing it.

When we think about threats to the environment, we tend to picture cars and smokestacks, not dinner. But the truth is, our need for food poses one of the biggest dangers to the planet. Agriculture is among the greatest contributor to global warming, emitting more greenhouse gases than all our cars, trucks, trains, and airplanes combined—largely from methane released by cattle and rice farms, nitrous oxide from fertilized fields, and carbon dioxide from the cutting of rain forests to grow crops or raise livestock. Farming is the thirstiest user of our precious water supplies and a major polluter, as runoff from fertilizers and manure disrupt fragile lakes, rivers, and coastal ecosystems across the globe.

To feed the estimated 9 billion people that we will soon be, we need to find new ways to produce protein as the environmental strain of industrial animal production becomes

---

50   Cited by Mark Bowen in his article "The Messenger." *Technology Review*, July/August 2006. P 38.
51   A colleague of Keeling. Roger Revelle had warned President Lyndon Johnson of the mounting crisis.

untenable. Beef produced in concentrated feeding operations typically requires nearly eight times the water and 160 times the land per calorie as vegetable and grain. A revolutionary biochemical industry is born. Meat is out, and plants are in. No animals necessary.

The environmental challenges posed by agriculture are huge, and they will only become more pressing as we try to meet the growing need for food worldwide. We will likely have 2 billion more mouths to feed by mid-century, but sheer population growth is not the only reason we'll need more food. The spread of prosperity across the world, especially in China and India, is driving an increased demand for meat, eggs, and dairy, boosting pressure to grow more corn and soybeans to feed more cattle, pigs, and chickens. If these trends continue, the double whammy of population growth and richer diets will require us to roughly double the number of crops we grow by 2050.

Unfortunately, the debate over addressing the global food challenge has become polarized pitting conventional agriculture and global commerce against local food systems and organic farms. The arguments can be fierce, and like our politics, we seem to be getting more divided rather than finding common ground. Those who favor conventional agriculture talk about modern mechanization, irrigation, fertilizers, and plant breeding, which they assert, can increase yield to help meet demand. Meanwhile, proponents of local and organic farms counter that the word's smaller farmers could increase yield plenty—and help themselves out of poverty—by adopting techniques that improve fertility without synthetic fertilizers and pesticides

But it does not appear to be an either/or proposition. Both approaches offer badly needed solutions; neither one alone get us there. We would be wise to explore all the good ideas, whether from organic and local farms or high tech conventional farms, and blend the best of both.

For most of our history, whenever we need to produce more food, we simply cut down forests or plowed grasslands to make more farms. But we can no longer afford to increase food production through agricultural expansion. Cutting down tropical forests is one of the most destructive things we can do to the environment, and it rarely benefits the 850 million people in the world who are still hungry. Most of the land cleared for agriculture in the tropics does not contribute much to the world's food security but is instead used to produce cattle, soybeans for livestock, timber, and palm oil. Avoiding further deforestation must be a top priority. Trees are the most important plants to absorb carbon dioxide to make carbohydrates through the process of photosynthesis.[52]

Thousands of years ago, human farming activities determined the trend for greenhouse gases by forcing their concentrations to rise when we should have driven them lower.[53] The temperature of the Earth—which profoundly affects the environment's suitability for life—is certain to rise as the amount of carbon dioxide in the air increases.

We have to decrease greenhouse gas concentrations, a task that requires the whole world to work in concert. We know how to solve the problem of global warming: use a combination of renewable energy sources including solar, wind, and hydropower plants. Many countries are on the

---

52   Yet, in 2019, fires have been deliberately set to clear the Amazon forest and transforming into agricultural lands.
53   William F. Ruddiman. *Plows, Plagues, and Petroleum How Humans) to reach the Took Control of Climate* (Princeton: Princeton University Press, 2010).

right track. For example, Portugal gets 100 percent of its electricity that way. [54]

Few are aware of the harmful effects of sulfur dioxide, a gas sent into the atmosphere and transformed into tiny sulfate particles called aerosols. Unlike sulfur from volcanic explosions, these particles do not reach the stratosphere, where they could remain for a few years before settling out, they rise to heights of a few hundred or thousand meters and slowly drift away in the prevailing winds from the points of emission. These particles are thought to have a regional scale cooling effect. William Ruddiman, a climate scientist for more than forty years, warns us that it may be a mistake to roll back both the greenhouse and smokestack emissions too abruptly because it would intensify the greenhouse warming for a while, before reducing it. It will take more than a century for the ocean to absorb half of the industrial carbon dioxide that now resides in the atmosphere.[55] We need new technologies to prevent global warming. Some wonder what the cost of these technologies will be, but that is not the important question. The real question is, "Will we be wise and smart enough to survive global warming?"

Global warning is affecting all species on land and sea, but differently. Although the increasing amount of greenhouse gases is a danger for humans and animals, it might not be for plants. Scientists say poison ivy is becoming more plentiful and potent—and the global increase in carbon dioxide is to blame.[56] Carbon dioxide acts like an airborne fertilizer, pushing plants to photosynthesize more and grow faster.

---

54   Maureen Hand. "Wind on the Upswing," *MIT Technology Review* November-December 2016, p 11.
55   William Ruddiman. Op cited, p 158.
56   Karen E. Lange Extra –Itchy Ivy. *National Geographic Magazine*, June 2008, p 25.

It is reasonable to think that if this is true for poison ivy, it might be true for all plants. It has been shown that increasing carbon dioxide in a greenhouse increases plant growth.

A commonly brought up solution to reducing carbon dioxide is planting more trees. Some organizations, such as Nature Conservancy, even do this.[57] But covering the planet with forests would not solve our problem.

However, physicist Klaus Lackner thinks he has a better idea: suck carbon dioxide out of the air with artificial trees that would operate at a thousand times the rate of real ones.[58] These artificial trees do not exist yet, but in Lackner's lab at Columbia University he and colleague Allen Wright are experimenting with bits of whitish-beige plastic that you might call artificial leaves. The plastic is a resin of the kind used to pull calcium out of water in a water softener. When Lackner and Wright impregnate that resin with sodium carbonate, it pulls carbon dioxide out of the air. The extra carbon converts the sodium carbonate to bicarbonate, or baking soda.[59]

Carbon dioxide scrubbers that rely on similarly simple chemistry already recycle human exhalations in submarines and space shuttles. Devising an economic way of scrubbing the outside air, though, is harder. But Lackner and Wright are busy working on that project, and no one can know if this idea will work until they've tried it. Can enough artificial trees be constructed to make a dent in climate change? And what happens to all the carbon dioxide they collect? Di-

---

57 *Nature Conservancy* (Michigan) Spring 2019, p 13.
58 See also Herve Ratel. Les Promesses e la feuillle artificiele. Scienxe er Vie. May 2011 See also James Temple. Is Carbon removal crazy or critical? *MIT Technology Review.* March April 2019. p 28.
59 Robert Kunzing. "Scrubbing the Skies," *National Geographic Magazine,* August 2010. p 30.

rect capturing and recycling of carbon dioxide is a very good idea, but so far not practical.[60]

Another approach to capture carbon dioxide is to boost crop yields by improving the process of photosynthesis. The idea came from the observation that in the hot springs of Yellowstone National Park, layers of colorful bacteria grow in thick mats. Near he water's surface, the green organisms photosynthesize like green plants do, using light and chlorophyll to split water molecules and make sugar. Farther down in the mats, the organisms are black. Botanists long assumed that they were incapable of photosynthesizing because they don't have access to enough visible light. And yet, on the very bottoms of the mats is a layer of green where no green should be. This means that the bacteria are using near infrared light to photosynthesize. A discovery which led to a growing body of research to improve crop yields by genetic engineering. The goal is to design a leaf canopy in crops that absorbs visible light in the upper leaves while using lower shady leaves to absorb the infrared light that passes through to ground level.

Storing energy from the sun by mimicking photosynthesis is something scientists have been trying to do since the early 1970s. Particularly, they have tried to replicate the way green plants break down water. Chemists, of course, can already split water. But the process requires high temperatures, harsh alkaline solution, or rare and expensive catalysts such as platinum. But in 2008, an MIT chemist, Daniel Nocera, demonstrated that with the help of a catalyst he developed, he could split a water molecule into oxygen and hydrogen.

Since then he has performed this solar process at efficiencies of greater than 10 percent, His artificial leaf was named

---

60   James Temple. "Is Carbon Removal Crazy or Critical?" *MIT Technology Review*, March-April 2019, p 28.

by *Time Magazine* as innovation of the year in 2011. He has elaborated this invention to accomplish a complete artificial photosynthetic cycle. The world is waiting for the commercialization of Nocera's bionic leaf.

4

A Note to the Reader

[In the spring of 2018] a team of economists reported that there was a 35 percent change that the United Nations' previous "worst case scenario" for global warming was in fact too optimistic. In January 2019 scientists concluded that the Earth's oceans were warming 40 percent faster than previously believed.

Bill McKibben

If the reader thinks that my book is pessimistic, he or she should read Nathaniel Rich's book, *Losing Earth: A Recent History*. Rich tells us that we missed the opportunity to stop climate change. It was a time—in the late 1970s—when minds were more open to change, when scientists had more influence, when the fuel industry was not as powerful as it is today. The last twenty years has emphasized the complexity of the Earth's climate to divide the public and immobilize our politics. If we do not respond to the threat of climate change in time, we will not survive. Other books on this topic that may be of interest include *The Great Derangement: Climate Change and the Unthinkable* by Amitav Ghosh; *We're Doomed: Now What?* by Roy Scranton; *The Uninhabitable Earth: Life after*

Warming by David Wallace Wells; and *Has the Human Game begun to play itself out?* by Bill McKibben.

The Uninhabitable Earth taps into the underlying emotion of the day: fear. This book is meant to scare the hell out of us because the severity of the situation still hasn't sufficiently registered in the minds of the public. Even Jim Hansen of NASA was unable to fully persuade people with his electrifying 1988 congressional testimony, where he explained that we have trashed the atmosphere. In the last few years, people have become more aware of climate change because they have witnessed terrible floods, monstrous hurricanes, melting glaciers, abnormal rainfalls, and invasions of seashores by oceans. However, people are not well-aware enough of the rapidity with which these events are occurring. According to Wallace-Wells, in the past three decades and since Al Gore published his first book on climate, more than half of the carbon dioxide exhaled into the atmosphere by burning fossil fuels has been emitted.[61] One wonders if Al Gore had been elected president of the U.S. instead of George W. Bush, if we would be in such a dire situation.

David Wallace's book is full of bad news and does not offer any solutions. But what could he say? We now burn 80 percent more coal than we did in 2000. Though solar energy costs have fallen 80 percent in that period and its use is growing worldwide, solar energy isn't eating away at fossil fuel use… just buttressing it. To the market, this is growth; to human civilization, it is almost suicide."[62]

So how do we go on? That has been Bill McKibben's concern ever since the publication in 1989 of *The End of Nature*. Its

---

61   David Wallace-Wells. *The Inhabitable Earth*. (New York: Tim Dungan Books, 2019), p 4.
62   Ibid, p 178.

premise is that since humans altered the entirety of Earth's atmosphere, there is truly no pristine nature left. In his recent book, *Falter*, McKibben describes just how much trouble we are in. He is a little more optimistic than Wallace-Wells, but not much.[63] To me, his chapters 6 and 7 are the most interesting because they tell us about the politics of climate change. On one side were the scientists who were telling us that we were facing the worst crisis of our history and on the other side are the climate deniers, who work mostly in the petroleum industry. But what I did not know was that fossil fuel corporations knew that they were poisoning the atmosphere and heating the Earth for decades before it was brought to light. We can compare the petroleum industry and the tobacco Industry. Both kill people, but it was far easier to solve the tobacco problem—stop smoking—than to solve the climate change problem. After all, fossil fuels are at the center of the world's economy—involved in every moment of a modern day—and yet are is the very things that are killing us.

A landmark U.N. report released on August 8, 2019 warns that humans now face a moment of reckoning over the way we use the planet's land: either we change our ways, particularly our diets, or risk devoting huge swaths of land to uses that spew far more carbon dioxide than we can afford. The report, authored by more than 100 scientists from 52 countries on the Intergovernmental Panel on Climate Change (IPCC), the U.N. climate science body found that emissions from land-use practices like agriculture and logging—cause nearly a quarter of human-induced greenhouse emissions. A global shift from meat-based to plant-based diets could yield big results, cutting as much as 8 billion metric tons of green-

---

63 Bill McKibben, *Falter: Has the Human Game Begun to Play Itself Out?* (Henry Holt and Company, 2019).

house gases per year. That's more than the annual emission of the entire U.S. Eating less meat means lower emissions from livestock and the fertilizer needed to grow their food, and offers the chance to reforest land that would have farmers otherwise used for grazing.

Another pessimistic book on climate change has been written in French by Fred Vargas.[64] This recent book has not been yet translated in English.[65] But, fortunately for me, who is a French native, I was able to read it. And here is a small review.

In her book Vargas paints the world as it will be if we do not do anything about the heating of the earth that continues to increase every day She blames our inactivity (or very little activity) on our governments which are run by politicians

Our politicians are more interested in making money than saving the planet. They are more interested in being reelected than they are in saving us (and them) from disaster. But, their money and power will have no worth when our civilization is gone. Vargas insists throughout her book that we have the power to change the course of our future by voting the politicians out. For Vargas humanity is in peril not only because of the danger of greenhouse gases, but also because we are going to run out of rare and so not rare minerals, such as iron and copper. We need also to recycle water that we waste.

---

64   Fred Vargas, *L'humanite en peril. Virons de bord toute!* Paris. Flamarion, 2019).

65   Fred Vargas's book is not written in classic French, but is full of slang expressions that require the reader to be a native Frenchman or French woman, or someone who have lived in France for many years. to understand the irony of the author. The translation of this book is a challenge. I would not attempt it.

In the last pages of her book, Fargas is more optimistic. She summarized what we should do to prevent our death-a lot- but we have to do it now, and altogether. Unfortunately, this is not forthcoming.

On Tuesday September 12, 2019 there was a debate between presidential democratic candidates. Although two or three candidates mentioned climate change, none gave us the impression that it was the primary thing on their mind. It should have been because the political and social problems which they discussed would disappear if we do not stop immediately the heating of our planet. If we don't do anything-or too little, I repeat, our death is certain.

5

Nuclear War

"A little bomb like that," said the famous physicist Enrico Fermi, cupping his hands as he looked over Manhattan, "and it would disappear."

Nuclear weapons are unique in their destructive power, in the unspeakable human suffering they cause, in the impossibility of controlling their effects in space and time, and in the threat they pose to the environment to future generations, and indeed to the survival of humanity.
International Committee of the Red Cross, 2010

Pollution and climate change are not the only deadly dangers the world faces —a nuclear war could destroy all life on Earth within a few minutes. The dawn of nuclear war was August 6, 1945. That day, the morning sun was warming the small streets of the big harbor of Hiroshima. The clock at Shima hospital struck 8:15 a.m., and no one was paying attention to an American plane hovering 9 kilometers above them and then disappearing. No one saw that it left a mortal package weighing 4 tons. At 580 meters, after a fall of 43 seconds, the bomb, *Little Boy*, exploded in blinding light. The plane's crew, dumfounded—ignored the real nature of the bomb and observed a terrifying cloud that growing into a mushroom shape and wiping out the city in a few seconds. It took around ten seconds for the fireball to reach its maximum size, releasing vast amounts of energy in the form of blast, heat, and radiation, killing hundreds thousand of people close to ground zero and causing lung injuries, ear damage, and internal bleeding further away.[66] People sustained injuries from collapsing buildings and thermal radiation was so intense that almost everything close to ground zero was vaporized. The extreme heat caused severe burns and ignited fires over a large area, which coalesced into a giant firestorm.

A second bomb was dropped three days later on Nagasaki, killing a further 100,000 Japanese. Buildings were transformed into rubble in seconds by the blast wave, and the high temperatures seared skin off, or blistered it so badly that it came off entirely when the person was moved. In both cities radiation was so intense that the offspring of survivors born *after the explosion* had chromosome and gene mutations affecting their health.[67]

We have now perfected the art of killing.[68] Throughout

---

66   The dropping of the atom bomb on Hiroshima and Nagasaki in 1945 was not justified as indispensable for victory which was then absolutely certain, but as a means of saving American soldiers' lives. But according to Gar Alperowitz in his book Atomic Diplomacy based on extensive research into the diaries of important political leaders involved in the decision to drop the bombs, the decision was a political move aimed at the Soviet Union.

67   See James Neel's work. Neel, at the University of Michigan, was one the first (medical) human geneticists.
68   J. Robert Oppenheimer's words as he watched the first atomic bomb test: "Now I become death, the destroyer of worlds."

our history we have killed each other with increasingly deadlier tools. First it was with rocks, then swords, bullets, ordinary bombs, and finally today with nuclear weapons that kill
a lot of people within a few seconds. Our attitude toward
nuclear war is a paradox. We have prevented further nuclear
war, because we are fearful of it. Yet we continue to arm ourselves to the teeth with nuclear weapons, hoping to deter our
enemies from attacking us.[69] Few of us realize that our modern atomic bombs are so powerful that the fallout of only one
or two is enough to destroy all of us, including life around
us. And so we continue to spend billions of dollars developing better, but useless, nuclear weapons. I agree with Eric
Schlosser: "As government officials in Washington, Moscow,
London, Paris, Beijing, New Delhi, Islamabad, Tel Aviv, and
Pyongyang discuss how to update and improve their arsenals, the madness at the heart of the whole enterprise must
be loudly asserted. How much is enough? The only rational
answer is even one nuclear weapon is too many."[70]

The growing danger of the nuclear-arms race has failed
to inspire much debate. Nuclear policy is not discussed in the
media: the public has been told little about the subject which
is of life and death importance. It may be because the details
of armaments are top secret. But I believe that may be another
reason for that incomprehension is that nuclear weapons are
based on atomic physics which is an unfamiliar science that
is restricted to scientists who have a fertile imagination. Until
roughly the end of the 19th century, when the universe could

---

69 During the Cold War the leaders did not have any illusions
about the value of nuclear missiles. As instruments of war such
weapons were uniquely unhelpful. Nonetheless, as a deterrent
device a nuclear arsenal had its uses if your opponent could be
convinced that it might ultimately be used.
70 See footnote 16.

still be described as a well behaved, deterministic mechanism of moving "billiard balls" (atoms/molecules), it was possible to talk of it in common sense terms; at least one was not required to stretch one's imagination beyond reasonable limits. But the picture changed. Our most basic concepts, upon which we build of all science, became so abstract as to defy simple, common scientific understanding. To make matters worse, from the point of view of the general public, determinism in science gave way to probability, and the universe might now be viewed, in a sense, as a cosmic game of chance.

However, you do not need a PhD in physics to understand the deadly dangers of an atomic bomb and where its incredible energy comes from. All you need is some knowledge about atoms, which I have summarized in Appendix 1 and some knowledge of the history of the atomic bomb.

History of the atom bomb

The concept of such a powerful bomb was born when physicists at the beginning of the 20th century discovered that the nucleus of an atom harbors unimagined energy and that it might be possible to find a way to unlock it and harness it.

In 1903 the British scientists, Ernest Rutherford and Frederic Soddy, estimated the astonishing quantity of energy locked up in the atom, in comparison to which the energy released by any chemical process, such as the detonation of an explosive, is at least 20,000 times more. "Suppose," Rutherford mused, "one could find a detonator to expel all this atomic energy at once: then some fool in a laboratory might blow up the universe unawares."[71] And as to Soddy, he ex-

---

71   Philip Ball. *Serving the Reich: The Struggle for the Soul of Physics under Hitler* (London: The Bodley Head, 2013), p 147.

pressed the same idea in a famous lecture in 1904: "The man who puts his hand on the lever by which a parsimonious nature regulates so jealously the output of this store of energy would possess a weapon by which he could destroy the earth if he chose."[72]

Another English physicist, Francis Ashton, who devised the mass spectrometer, is reported to have said in 1919, "To change the hydrogen in a glass of water into helium would release enough energy to drive the Queen Mary across the Atlantic and back at full speed." [73]

Such a release amount of energy is due to what we now call nuclear fission, which is the splitting of an atom's nucleus. Nuclear fission can occur naturally or artificially (by bombarding the nucleus of the atom with neutrons).

Nuclear fission of heavy elements was discovered on December 17, 1938 by the German physicist Otto Halm and his assistant Fritz Strasman and explained theoretically in January 1939 by Lise Meitner and her nephew Otto Robert Frish. It is an exothermic reaction which can release large amounts of energy both as electromagnetic radiation and as kinetic energy. It was assumed that natural fission did not exist or was insignificant. But it exists on a small scale. This was discovered in 1940 by the Russian physicists Flyorov Perzhak and Igor Kurchatov, when they decided to confirm that, without bombardment by neutrons, the fission rate of uranium was indeed negligible. It was not. The idea that fission occurs spontaneously was reinforced later.[74]

All the physicists before World War II understood that

---

72   Ibid., 148.
73   Ibid., 151
74   "The Workings of an Ancient Nuclear Reactor," *Scientific American.* January 26, 2009.

atomic energy might be tapped one day, but they were sure that such prospect was indefinitely remote. Yet, it took only one generation to go from the discovery of atomic structure to the obliteration of Hiroshima and Nagasaki.[75] On January 25, 1939, a team of physicists at Columbia University used the cyclotron[76] to split an atom of uranium for the first time on American soil.

In the minds of scientists, the discovery of fission had two practical applications, both at odds with each other: a peaceful source of energy and an incredible force of destruction. "Complementary" was the word that the physicist Niels Bohr used to describe the contradiction inherent in quantum physics—and philosophically in life itself.[77]

A nuclear reaction could light a city.

A nuclear reaction could level a city.

It was all a matter of how the energy was used.

Nuclear fission can produce energy for nuclear power or drive the explosion of nuclear weapons. Both uses are pos-

---

75   In 1914 H.G. Wells wrote his book *The World Set Free* after looking into the future forecast by Soddy, Rutherford and Ashton, into which humankind had learnt how to liberate nuclear energy. In the book Wells wrote of a war between England, France and America on one side, and Germany and Austria on the other, beginning in 1956. It would use what Wells called 'atomic bombs' which would destroy all the major cities of the world.

76   A cyclotron is an apparatus in which charged atomic and subatomic are accelerated by alternating electric fields while following an outward spiral or circular path in a magnetic field.

77   There is a whole new branch of physics called quantum mechanics that now accommodates a vast amount of experimental material in both physics and chemistry and has been as fruitful as any development in the history of the physical sciences. Quantum mechanics was born out of the concept that light can be a particle and a wave in the same time; which is seemingly a paradox.

sible because certain substances undergo fission when struck by neutrons, and in turn emit neutrons when they break apart. This makes a self-sustaining nuclear chain reaction possible, releasing energy at a very rapid, uncontrolled rate in a nuclear weapon; or a controlled rate in a nuclear reactor. However, accidents can occur like at Three Mile Island (United States), Chernobyl (Russia), or Fukushima (Japan). The Three Mile Island accident was a meltdown at a nuclear power plant near Middletown, Pennsylvania. It occurred on March 28, 1979. Officially it caused no deaths. But unofficial investigations and lawsuits claimed there were above average rates of cancer and birth defects in the surrounding areas.

But the other accidents were far more serious. They brought death and desolation and were blamed on technology and lack of safety culture.[78]

In the early hours of April 26, 1986, reactor number four at the Chernobyl nuclear station suffered a massive power surge, resulting in a fire and the release of four hundred times more radioactive material than the atomic bomb dropped on Hiroshima. The reactor had been built in the 1970s with severe breaches. According to Arkady Ostrovsky,[79] the only reason it passed an inspection by foreign experts was that prior to the inspection, its engineers had temporarily replaced Soviet electronics with Swedish and American ones.

Carelessness, the lack of regard for life, and cover up were the reasons for the disaster. After Chernobyl, the world had a preview of what would happen if nuclear weapons are used.

The idea of building an atomic bomb was born in the

---

78   Nuclear lessons. *MIT Technology Review.* July-August 2011. p 8.
79   Arkady Ostrovsky. *The Invention of Russia* (New York: Viking, 2015), p 62.

mind of Leo Szilard, a Hungarian physicist and refugee living in the U.S., who realized that progress in nuclear physics would lead not only to new sources of energy but also to conceive bombs of unheard power. Szilard was very worried that the Nazis would build an atomic bomb before the Allies.[80] He convinced Albert Einstein to write a letter to President Roosevelt in August 1939 suggesting that the United States immediately start such a project. In 1941 Roosevelt gave the go ahead and the first atomic bomb exploded in the Alamagordo desert in New Mexico in 1945 demonstrating a destructive power more frightening than anyone could imagine.

The energy released by atomic bombs cannot be overemphasized. Even the first fission bombs were thousands of times more explosive than a comparable mass of chemical explosive. Little Boy weighed a total of about four tons (of which 60 kg was nuclear fuel) and was 11 feet (3.4 m) long. It also yielded an explosion equivalent to about 15 kilotons of TNT. Modern nuclear weapons are hundreds of times more energetic for their weight than the first pure fission atomic bombs. A single modern nuclear weapon weighing less than 1/8 of Little Boy's weight has a yield of 475,000 tons of TNT, and could bring destruction to about 10 times the area of Hiroshima. The amount of free energy contained in nuclear fuel is millions of times the amount of free energy contained in a similar mass of chemical fuel such as gasoline.

---

80   Essentially it is now clear that Nazi Germany failed to make a nuclear bomb not because German scientists did not know it could be made, or try to make it, with degree of reluctance, but because the German war-machine was unwilling or unable to devote the necessary resources to it. They abandoned the effort and switched to what seemed the more cost effective concentration on rocketry, which promise quicker returns.

In 1949 the Soviets managed to explode their first atomic bomb. Then France, Great Britain, and China joined the club of atomic powers. A few years later, Israel, India, and Pakistan had their own atomic bombs.

Once the U.S.S.R. acquired nuclear weapons—four years after Hiroshima— the superpowers realized that the use of such nuclear weapons would lead to suicide. Yet, they continued to build deadlier weapons. The United States' nuclear arsenal grew rapidly through the 1950s. From 9 in 1946, to 50 in 1948 and 170 by the beginning of the next decade. The stockpile of nuclear weapons at the disposal of the U.S. armed forces had reached 841 by 1952 before expanding to around 2,000 by the time of Germany's entry into NATO. It would reach 28,000 on the eve of the Cuban Missile Crisis seven years later.

To deliver these bombs, the U.S. Air Force had a fleet of about 50 forward-based B-29 bombers from the onset of the 1948 Berlin blockade to well over 1,000 five years later; the first intercontinental B-52 bombers entered service in June 1955. Given the Soviet Union's overwhelming advantage in manpower and convention weapons in Europe, these airborne nuclear weapons inevitably became central to Washington's strategy, especially following President Truman's secret order on March 10, 1950, to accelerate the development of a hydrogen bomb.

In a hydrogen bomb, far more powerful than an atomic bomb, two isotopes of hydrogen, deuterium and tritium are fused to form a nucleus of helium and a neutron. This fusion requires a lot of energy that is supplied by the explosion of a fission atomic bomb. In other words, a hydrogen bomb is made up of two atomic bombs: a fission atomic bomb and a fusion atomic bomb. The advent of the hydrogen bomb seemed to endanger no less than the future of humanity. The new weapons could be made hundreds, if not thousands, of times more powerful than the bomb that destroyed Hiroshima. Fortunately for us no hydrogen bomb has ever exploded.

Yet, the threat of nuclear war appeared from time to time on the horizon. For example, at the height of the Cold War, the Cuban Missile Crisis of 1962 almost plunged the world into an unnecessary war for a few days. It frightened even the top decision-makers into rationality for a while.[81] Nevertheless, since 1945, we are on the edge of a precipice clinging to a few bushes.[82]

The nuclear dilemma hangs like a giant question mark over us... Throughout the cold war, there was a nuclear arms race between the U.S. and the U.S.S.R and chances to eliminate nuclear weapons were minimal. It was the era of deterrence. In the first years of the post-cold war, the nuclear peril seemed all but disappear. People, including presidents, associated the fact that the Soviet Union had ended with the idea that there was no more danger of using nuclear weapons. "I saw the chances to rid our children's dreams of the nuclear nightmare, and I did," President George W. Bush said at the Republican convention in 1992; and in 1997, President Bill Clinton boasted that, "our children are growing up free from the shadows of the cold war and the threat of nuclear holocaust."

For years, nuclear weapons all but dropped out of the

---

81   The Soviet leader, N.S. Khrushchev decided to place Soviet missiles in Cuba to offset the American missiles already in place across the Soviet border in Turley. Both countries withdrew their missiles.

82   When I was a child on the community of Roquebrune-Cap Martin, the villagers celebrated one day in the year their creed that a large amount of shrubs (local name: genets) prevented the old village to slide in the sea when an earthquake struck.

news and Americans were given little indication that some 31,000 nuclear weapons remained in the world, or that 7,000 of them were targeted at the United States. A whole generation came of age lacking even rudimentary information regarding nuclear arms and nuclear peril.[83] Nuclear policy is no longer widely discussed as it was after World War II. The public has been told little about this subject that involves their own existence. Few of us are asking the following questions: Why do we have nuclear weapons? What they are for? How might they be used?

Well, twenty years later we are back at the time when the Berlin Wall was demolished; Russia, the former Soviet Union, menaces Europe; and North Korea, menaces the United States. We are now in a second nuclear age with the same dangers we were confronted with in 1945, but with deadlier nuclear weapons and the knowledge that disarmament treaties do not work. Countries like North Korea can build nuclear weapons at will, including hydrogen bombs,[84] while other countries are busy developing better cruise missiles and launching ballistic-missile submarines. The use of these submarines is very important. Suppose that Russia or North Korea decide to use nuclear weapons and succeed in destroying New York City or the rest of United States, there is nothing to prevent a nuclear submarine (even a drone submarine) from destroying parts of Russia or North Korea. Hence, everyone in the world would be a victim of a modern nuclear war, no matter where it started. There is great danger because we have not found a way to intercept enemy in-

---

83   Including my grand children.
84   Eric Schlosser. The Growing Dangers of the New Nuclear-Arms Race, *The New Yorker.* May 24.

tercontinental ballistic missiles.[85] For more than a decade the
United States has been testing a system to intercept such missiles.[86] So far, this system has been unreliable. The interceptor
missiles cost billions of dollars and seemingly add to global
nuclear risks while offering minimal protection. [87] Could it be
that there is no way to protect ourselves against ICBMs? As I
said before, we have reached the zenith of killing each other.
Are we doomed to death? Or shall we learn to live in peace?

---

85   An international ballistic missile ICBM, is a guided ballistic
minimum range of 5,500 kilometers (34000 miles) primarily designed for nuclear weapons delivery.
86   Laura Gregor and David Wright. "Broken Shields," *Scientific
American*, June 2019, p 62.
87   Ibid.

6

I Am Worried

The abolition of war has become not only desirable but absolutely necessary if the planet is to be saved. It is an idea whose time has come.

Howard Zinn

Just after the dropping of the two atomic bombs on Japan in 1945, some of us still in uniform asked the question: "Are wars over after the invention and the use of atomic bombs? " At the time the answer was not clear, but more than 70 years later we can say that nuclear weapons have not been used again in combat since 1945, and they did prevent global wars as World War I and II. On the other hand they have not prevented civil wars or wars between nations that did not have nuclear weapons. What they also did was to instigate more conflict. For example, the mere rumor of a nuclear program in Iraq—and the thought of Saddam Hussein supplying his nukes to terrorists[88]—was enough to send the United States

---

88   Although the basic facts about building nuclear weapons were no longer secret since 1945, it is not simple to build an atomic bomb; you need a lot of financial and technological resources and even,

into a costly war that has gone since 2003. That war could have been prevented because Hussein did not have nuclear weapons.

People react differently to the idea of an atomic war. Some, like atomic scientists, believe that the next war, if nuclear weapons are used, would be the last one. [89] Some nation leaders shared that opinion. President Eisenhower was one of them. He wrote a letter to Winston Churchill in the spring of 1956 in which he says:

> It would be unsafe to predict that, if the West and the East should ever become locked up in a life and death struggle, both sides would still have sense enough not to use this horrible instrument. [90]

Another leader was Khrushchev who was entirely rational about the use of nuclear weapons. His aversion to war was genuine. He wrote to President Kennedy on October 26, at the height of the Cuba crisis:

> If indeed war would break out, then it would not be in our power to stop it, for such is the logic of war, I have participated in two wars and I know that war ends when it has rolled through cities and villages, everywhere sowing death and destruction. [91]

---

if a terrorist group could get sufficient enriched uranium to make a bomb, they might not be able to make an efficient atomic bomb. According to experts in the field, there are a lot of things that could go wrong.

89   See the *Bulletin of the Atomic Scientists*.

90   Quoted by Bret Baier in *Three Days in January*. (New York: Harper Collins: 2017), p 190.

91   Anatoly Dobkrin. *In Confidence* (Time Books, 1995), p 46.

On the other hand Barry Goldwater as presidential candidate in 1964 had pledged to do whatever it took to win the Vietnam War even suggesting the use of "low yielding atomic weapons to block the infiltration of North Vietnamese troops and supplies into South Vietnam. It did not strike every one as a nutty idea. Hanson Baldwin, the military editor of the New York Times, offered a supportive column claiming that a single "nominal yield" atomic bomb could "clear" as much forest as twenty –five million pounds of napalm."[92]

Fortunately for humanity, it has been realized hat as instruments of war nuclear weapons are unhelpful. Nonetheless, as a deterrent they played a peaceful role: they prevented to have a war between the great powers of the day. The U.S. and the Soviet Union decided to arm them to the hilt preparing for the eventuality of a nuclear war that never came.

Yet, in fact, the net result of this phase of mutual threats and brinkmanship was a relatively stabilized international system, and a tacit agreement of the two superpowers not to frighten each other. It was symbolized by the installation of a telephone "hot line" between the White House and the Kremlin in 1963 after the Cuban crisis. The leaders of the U.S. and the Soviet Union had finally realized the stupidity of building better and better nuclear weapons. But what could happen when world leaders are not as wise as Kennedy and Khrushchev in 1962 or George H. W. Bush and Michail Gobarchev when they signed the Intermediate-Range Nuclear Treaty in 1987.

I do not have a problem with the idea of atomic weap-

---

92 See Christian Appy. *American Reckoning* (New York: Viking, 2015), p 9.

ons as a deterrent, but with the excessive number of nuclear weapons you need to accomplish this. We need very few of them to kill our enemy—and ourselves at the same time. Yet today, the nine nuclear-armed nations spend tens of billions of dollars each year maintaining and modernizing their nuclear arsenals, a worthless military program that diverts public funds from health care, education, disaster relief and other vital services.

I am worried because, although the U.S. did not test a nuke since President George W. Bush declared a self imposed testing moratorium, President Donald Trump is convinced that the best way to limit the spread of nuclear danger is to expand and advertise the ability to annihilate one's enemies. He has signed off on a $ 1.2 trillion plan to overhaul the entire nuclear-weapons complex.[93] Trump like many others believe that the nation that has the most and the best nuclear weapons will win the war. But, in a nuclear war, there are no winners. We are all losers because, I repeat, all of us will be dead

I am worried because established nuclear powers are modernizing their arsenals.[94] For example Vladimir Putin, the Russian President, in his 2018 annual address to the Federal Assembly unveiled a generation of nuclear weapons,[95] each capable to destroy every American city with a population larger than a million people. [96] France and the United Kingdom are developing replacements for their Vangard and Triumphant ballistic-missile submarines. China is introducing Dongfeng-41 warheads ballistic missiles that will be mounted on trucks, loaded with up to ten nuclear warheads, and ca-

---

93   *Time*, "The Nuclear Poker." February 12, 2018, p 22.
94   *Time*, February 2018, p 21.
95   *Time*, April 2018, p 40.
96   Eric Schlosser. "The Growing Dangers of the New Nuclear-Arms Race." *The New Yorker*, May 24, 2018.

pable of reaching anywhere in the United States.[97] Pakistan now has the world's fastest-growing nuclear stockpile. Israel is expanding the range of its Jericho III ballistic missiles and deploying cruise missiles with nuclear weapons on submarines.[98]

I am worried because other countries want to belong to the atomic club. Iran is one. The other is North Korea that since 2017 seriously menaces the U.S., South Korea, and Japan with its new arsenal of nuclear weapons. In November of that year, North Korea tested what experts assess to be true two-stage thermonuclear device: [99] it tested the Hwasong-15 missile, which experts believe has a range of 8,000 kilometers, the Korean "president" Kim Jong Un wanted to be seen on equal footing with other powerful nations and ultimately secure a guarantee that the U.S. won't attack and will eventually leave the Korean Peninsula. And that is in great part what Kim got after the meeting he had with President Trump on June 12, 2018 in Singapore. In late February 2019 Kim and Trump met again, this time in Hanoi (Vietnam). The meeting was short and a complete failure. President Trump left Hanoi without signing anything. Within days of the summit satellite imaginary showed that Kim was rebuilding some of North Korea's rocket facilities. The reason is simple. North Korea is not going to give up its nuclear deterrent. Beyond their military utility, nuclear weapons are all that North Korea has to command international attention. The only hope we have is that Kim is bluffing and had no real intention to use his nuclear weapons knowing that to do that is to sign his own death sentence and the one of everybody else.

---

97   Ibid.
98   Ibid.
99   Which might be an hydrogen bomb.

To me the most astonishing thing that Trump came up about these meetings was what he said to *Time*. "If I can save millions of lives coming here [Singapore], sitting down and establishing a relationship with someone who's a very powerful man, who's got firm control of a country and that country has very powerful nuclear weapons, it is my honor to do it."[100] In other words Trump is conscious how deadly a nuclear war would be, but he does not realize that he could be himself a victim since any nuclear weapon (Korean or not) can destroy Washington and the White House with it.

I am worried because politicians and others speak about the death of human beings as if they were mosquitoes. For example on October 1961 President Kennedy secretly met with military advisers at the White House to discuss the pros and the cons of launching a nuclear surprise attack on the Soviet Union. American and Soviet troops were confronting each other in Berlin and a war between the Superpowers seemed possible. Kennedy wanted to hear the benefits of striking first. A Kennedy aide, Carl Kaysen had come up with a surprise attack plan, focusing solely on air bases and missile sites. He predicted that I would kill "less than 1,000,000, and probably not much more than 500,000."

I am worried because the dangers brewing on the Korean peninsula are not the only nuclear risks evident: the United States and Russia remained at odds, continuing military ex-

---

100 The Dare me Doctrine, President Trump defiant Doctrine, *Time* June 25, 2018, p 19. It is interesting to note that in the same article the author Brian Bennet mentions the possibility of the death of millions of people if Trump misplays his hand. It is indeed rare to find in the media the obvious concept that nuclear weapons would kill millions of lives.

ercises along the borders the borders of NATO, undermin-
ing the Intermediate-Range Nuclear Forces Treaty (INF), up-
grading their nuclear arsenals, and eschewing arms control
negotiations. In South Asia, Pakistan and India have continued to build ever-larger arsenals of nuclear weapons. And in
the Middle East uncertainty about the continued support for
the landmark Iranian nuclear deal adds to the black overall
picture. To call the world nuclear situation dire is to under-
state the danger—and its immediacy. The risk that nuclear
weapons may be used—intentionally or because of miscalcu-
lation—is growing fast.

Like Eric Chlosser. I am, worried, because (I am quoting
him):

> The growing danger of the nuclear arm race has failed
> to inspire much debate. Nuclear policy is no longer
> widely discussed in the media; the public has been
> told little about a subject of existential importance;
> and questions once passionately argued have been
> largely forgotten. Why do we have nuclear weapons?
> Why they are for? How can they be used? And at a
> time where a single American submarine can destroy
> the capital city of every country in the United Na-
> tions, how much is enough? [101]

I am worried because of the lack of comprehension on
the part of the government and the public of the dangers of
nuclear weapons. For example, on Saturday January 14, 2018,
there was a false alarm of a nuclear attack on Hawaii and
for 38 minutes people tried to hide in bathrooms, basements,
anywhere they could. They did not realize that if it had been

---

101   Ibid., p 2.

a real attack they would not have survived. The alert told the Hawaiians that "Ballistic Missile threat bound to Hawaii. Seek immediate shelter. This is not a drill. "The problem is that there is no shelter against nuclear weapons. The shelter that the people did seek, that fateful January 2018, dates from World 1 War against shells, not nuclear weapons. It seems that we are back in 1961 when we were trained to "duck and cover." We were told to build home shelters. School children performed drills where at the sound of an alarm they dropped and huddled beneath rickety wooden desks, hands over their heads. All this was a futile exercise.

I am worried because the use of nuclear weapons brings an instant catastrophe: no effective response exists and none can be imagined. This catastrophe would happen in a few minutes. According to nuclear security experts, it would not take more than five minutes for as many as 400 land-based nuclear weapons in the U.S. arsenal to be loosened on enemy targets after the initial "go" order. Ten minutes later a battalion of underwater nukes could join them. There is no way to recall the missiles when they are launched, and there is no self-destruct switch.

I am worried because the decision to use the atomic bomb in a conflict between the U.S.A. and some other country was for years in the hands or rather the mind of just one man. Before 1962, that man was General LeMay, former commander of the American bomber fleet that had aimed to destroy Japan's will to fight in 1945. As a matter of fact, when Kennedy administration arrived in 1961 no one in the White House knew that LeMay could decide when a nuclear attack on the

U.S.S.R was necessary, and what ought to be on the target list.[102] The idea that only one man decides when to use the atomic bomb in a war is not dead.

Today, the decision to strike is in the hands of the U.S. president and this unbridled decision is a frightening prospect no matter who is the president.[103] Yet, with exception of the president, every link in the U.S nuclear decision chain has protections against poor judgments, deliberate misuse or accidental deployment. There is no comparable restraint on the U.S. president. [104] I am worried because although the Atomic Energy Act of 1946 specified that the President has the sole authority to order the use of nuclear weapons, during the Eisenhower administration, the authority to use nuclear weapons was secretly delegated to relatively low-level officers who needed to defend themselves on the battlefield. Fortunately we were able to avoid wars between the U.S. and the Soviet Union or another nation. In 1974, Sam Nunn, chairman of the U.S. Committee on Armed Services, said after a tour of NATO's tactical nuclear units, "Nobody has any experience in fighting nuclear wars, and nobody knows what would happen if one were to start." The answer to Nunn's observation is that there is nothing one can do but hope that the day of a nuclear war never comes.

I am worried because there are myths concerning the use of nuclear weapons. The first one is "It is O.K. for some countries to possess nuclear weapons and not for others." The re-

---

102   Ibid., p 14.

103   To use the atomic bomb in 1945 was decided by one man, President Truman.

104   Nuclear war should require a second opinion. *Scientific American* August 2017, p 8.

ality is that when it comes to nuclear weapons, there are no safe hands. The second myth is that it is unlikely that nuclear weapons will ever be used again. The reality is that unless we eliminate nuclear weapons, they will almost certainly be used again, intentionally or by accident, and the consequences will be catastrophic. While many thousands of nuclear weapons have been dismantled since the end of the cold war, the justifications for maintaining them remain largely unchanged. Nations still cling to the misguided idea of "nuclear deterrence," when it is clear that nuclear weapons only cause national and global insecurity.[105]

I am a worrier like Daniel Ellsberg[106] because the White House and the media are talking about a nuclear war. as it was the same kind of war as World War I. They believe that "The more bombs we have, the more likely we will win it". As I said more than once before, this assumption has no basis because one or two modern atomic bombs are enough to destroy humanity and other living things. Yet, the concept, that the fallout of atomic bombs is terribly deadly not only for those who are targeted but also for those who witness such an explosion, seems to have been hard to grasp for the U.S. army. From July 1945, when the first atomic test was conducted in the New Mexico desert, to the end of atmospheric testing in 1963, the United States conducted 235 above ground

---

105 "Five Myths about Nuclear Weapons," *The Washington Post.* September 30, 2016.
106 Daniel Ellsberg copied and released a huge collection of secret documents about the Vietnam war, first published in June 1971 by the *New York Times*, which became known as the *Pentagon Papers.* He published a book in 2018, *The Doomsday Machine: Confession of a Nuclear War Planner.*

explosions on Pacific Islands and the Nevada desert. Between May and July 1956 there were 17 tests of bombs in the Marshall Islands that were hundreds of time as powerful as the Hiroshima bomb. Five different B-57B planes made 27 passes through the mushroom clouds to obtain radiation-dose information. For the pilots and crew, there was no medical followup. Naval officers aboard battleships ingested more plutonium in a bite of contaminated ham in the mess hall than it is considered acceptable exposure over the entire lifetime of a nuclear-plant worker.[107]

The largest-ever U.S. nuclear test, called Castle Bravo, was conducted in 1954 in the Pacific and was equal to 1,000 Hiroshima bombs. A vast storm of radioactive fallout poisoned both American military men and the people of the Marshall Islands, a smattering of atolls between Australia and Hawaii. [108]

During the congressional testimony in 1956 -57, an Army general recommended that the United States build and maintain a stockpile of 151,000 warheads for his branch alone, even though Operation Alert revealed that just one would flatten a metropolis. But another general, Dwight Eisenhower, said: "There just are not enough bulldozers to scrape off the bodies of the streets."[109] Nuclear weapons were also detonated by the Soviet Union near the Artic Circle and in present day Kazakhstan. Both countries should be condemned for not understanding that they kill people doing these tests.

The United Nations has sought to eliminate nuclear weapons ever since its establishment. The first resolution adopted by the UN General assembly in 1946 established a

---

107   Dan Zak, Almight (New York: Blue Ride Press), p 44.
108   Ibid., p 47.
109   Ibid., p 49.

commission to deal with problems related to the discovery of atomic energy among others. The Commission was to make proposals for the control of atomic energy to the extent necessary to ensure its use only for peaceful purposes. The resolution also decided that Commission should make proposals for "the elimination from national armaments of atomic weapons and all other major weapons adaptable to mass destruction. " Since then, a number of multilateral treaties have since been established with the aim of preventing nuclear proliferation, while promoting progress in nuclear disarmament. But treaties have to be respected. Most of the time, they are not. In the last few years there has been a slowdown in disarmament, which has spurred activists and nations to advocate for a treaty to ban nukes outright. But unfortunately the U.S. government—whose nuclear arsenal is the bedrock of its national security policy –is not in favor of the ban, viewing it as both unrealistic and potentially harmful to the long riding process of disarmament.

People of a certain age will remember the Doomsday Clock maintained by *the Bulletin of the Atomic Scientists*. It expressed the risk of nuclear annihilation as time remaining midnight. To day, the second hand has been pushed 30 second forward, the closest Doomsday has loomed since 1953, when the US and the Soviet Union first tested hydrogen bombs within months of each other.

Finally, I am worried because all technological advances have been used for war. The invention of airplanes brought a revolution in transportation, but permitting bombing of cities. The discovery that there is a fantastic amount of energy in atoms which could be harnessed led to atomic power plants, but also to nuclear weapons,. We use dynamite to build tunnels or destroy old buildings, but we destroy cities in time of war. The internet brought instant knowledge to everyone and instant communication between people with computers, but it also brought cyber warfare. There are good and bad consequences for every invention.[110] I wonder what we are going to invent something more deadly than nuclear weapons. I do not believe that we can, but I may be wrong. In any case it is time to realize that our technology to kill has reached the point of no return,: we cannot win wars, certainly not with nuclear weapons. We have to prevent wars. Will we succeed or shall we commit suicide?

---

110   DNA testing seems innocuous, but it may reveal family secrets. In just one among many such stories, a 23 and Me user who tested himself and his parents for a class he was teaching on genetics unearthed a half brother. The revelation "uncorked" emotions with his family, he wrote on vox.com, and his parents eventually divorced.

7

A Ray of Hope

To see what is in front of one's nose needs a constant struggle.

George Orwell

Although Hilary Clinton and Donald Trump did not face a single question about global warming during the 2016 debates, today with freakish wildfires, flooded coastlines and farm lands, daily tornadoes, and deadly hurricanes, the issue is seared in voters' minds. They are reminded of climate change every time they turn on their TVs or read their e-mails.

Some politicians say the 2020 presidential election will be the one which climate change finally breaks through. According to a survey by the Yale Program on Climate Communication, and a February 2018 poll from the Center for American progress suggests that the issue may be especially relevant in five early-voting states where Democratic primary voters rank climate as their top concern, alongside health care.

American cities are not waiting until the 2020 presidential election; they are attempting prevent what could be a very serious catastrophe. To quote Trevor Hughes:

On a sunny summer's day at Christopher Columbus Park on Boston's waterfront, it is hard to picture the dormant fury of the Atlantic Ocean as it laps softly at the creaking docks. But one day, a storm driven by unusually high winds and high tides will pour water over the park's grassy rise and inundate the arbors where grapevines trail and newlyweds pose for photos. The waters will rush across the brick pavers onto Atlantic Avenue and flow towards historic Faneuil Hall and Quincy Market, where generations of tourists have learned about the Boston Tea Party. The floodwaters will threaten nearby Old North Church, where Paul Revere's ride kicked off, and lap at the edges of Bunker Hill. High tides and strong already regularly inundate the area, but this storm would be different. It's a vision that keeps Boston Mayor Marty Walsh up at night. That is why Walsh is preparing to have the city, spend billions of dollars over the next decade to try to blunt the efforts of climate change on the city, including armoring Columbus Park and gently raising it up to provide a buffer against the worse of what the Atlantic can throw.[111]

Walsh is not alone. According to a survey of mayors, the majority of U.S. cities are planning to take climate related actions in 2019.

New York State aims to build "living" oyster–encrusted barriers on Staten Island for storm defense and ecological restoration to shield the highly vulnerable neighborhood of Tottenlville from storm waves similar to those of Hurricane

---

111   Trevor Hughes. "Climate Battle Now Local." *USA Today,* January 6, 2019.

Sandy.[112] But these barriers are not going to protect against rising seas.

Florida Representative Kathy Castor is confident that a special House committee on climate change will play a leading role on one of the most daunting challenges facing the planet. She says, "Congress has a 'moral obligation' to protect future generations from the costly effects of climate change, including more severe hurricanes, a longer wildfire season and a dangerous sea-level rise."[113] But it is not just Democrats who suddenly want to focus on climate change, Florida Congressman Matt Caetz, an ardent defender of President Trump, introduced a bill in 2017 to eliminate the EPA, but changed his mind and now believes climate change is real. In December 2018, John Cormyn of Texas, who recently served in GOP Senate leadership, tweeted positively about a tax on carbon emissions, and a month later, Republican Representative Francis Rooney of Florida and democratic colleagues joined together to introduce a carbon-tax measure in the House.[114] Note that these Representatives are all from Florida and have seen first hand the damage that the ocean can do in a series of hurricanes. They have finally realized that the effects of climate change will be catastrophic if global temperatures continue to rise. According to data from the Yale Program on Climate Change Communication, more than 70% of Americans now understand that climate change is taking place.[115] Let us hope that they can encourage Congress to act.

Climate change action taken by Congress may be pos-

---

112   "Breaking Waves," *Scientific American*, May 2019, p 14.
113   *Lansing State Journal*, Sunday, February 10, 2019, p 7A.
114   Justin Worland. "A New Climate for Climate." *Time*, April 1, 2019. p 31.
115   Ibid.

sible. In 2019, newly elected Representative Alexandria Oca-sio-Cortez of New York and Senator Ed Markey of Massachu-setts called for the U.S. to launch a broad program called *The Green New Deal*, to decarbonize the economy while tackling a slew of other social ills. The response was mixed. People loved it. People loathed it. Others were confused by it. But in the capital, where climate change has long been regarded as a low priority, lawmakers could no longer avoid the issue.

Hope to avoid the crisis of climate change stems largely from the recent, unprecedented groundswell of youth activism. The movement has been led by a 17-year-old Swedish student named Greta Thunberg, who captured the world's attention with a groundbreaking speech at the U.N.'s annual gathering of world leaders in Poland in 2018. Thunberg spoke with startling clarity about the threat her generation faces and how political leaders have failed the test of leadership. She said, "Why should we care about our future when no one else is doing that? And why should we should bother to learn the facts when facts don't matter in this society?"[116]

Today the young are showing us the way forward. Many have listened to Greta Thunberg's call to action. High school activists are marching in cities, challenging their leaders to act once and for all. But of course, individual action or group action will not be enough unless policy makers create the conditions for collective change.[117]

Jane Goodall recognized the power of young people and that many had been losing hope. To help encourage the former, she started the Roots & Shoots program in 1991, which

---

116   *Time*, September 23, 2019, p 48.
117   This book was finished when, on September 20, 2019, more than a million students around the world skipped classes to protest the lack of action on the part of governments regarding climate change.

allowed children of all ages to work on projects that make the world a better place for animals.[118]

Another area in which progress has been made is in fighting air pollution. Autonomous vehicles have been created to help decrease exhaust from cars and trucks. They have been tested for millions of miles on public roads, and pilot programs are underway for delivery and taxi services in places like the suburbs of Phoenix. But driverless cars are not ready to take over roads in general. They have trouble handling chaotic traffic and difficulty with weather conditions like snow and fog. Autonomous vehicles may allow a reimagining of transportation altogether if they can be made reliably safe. Private cars will not be as present on the road because people will be able to summon a driverless vehicle to take them wherever necessary. Traffic jams might be eliminated as well as parking problems. Above all, if widely deployed, self-driving cars are expected to eliminate most of the 1.25 million deaths a year caused by traffic accidents.

Progress is also being made in the field of renewable energy. Wind and solar power technology are becoming cheaper and more widely deployed, but they do not generate electricity when the sun is not shining or when the wind is not blowing. Those factors limit the supply of energy and how quickly we can move away from steady sources like coal and natural gas. We need batteries to store sun's power on a sunny day or the wind's power on a windy day, but those batteries are not as efficient and cheap as they could be. Even the best solar cells convert less than one-third of the energy from sunlight into electricity. When the sunlight strikes a solar cell, it normally produces some very high-energy elec-

118 Jane Goodall. The devastation of climate is real. But there are reasons to be hopeful. *Time*, September 23, 2019, p 50.

trons, but within a few trillionths of a second, those electrons shed most of their energy as heat. Researchers are working on new techniques which would make solar cells far more efficient, and less costly.

In any case, over the last decade 2009-2019, there has been a staggering fall in the price of solar and wind power, and of the lithium-ion batteries used to store energy. This has led to rapid expansion of these technologies, even though they are still used much less than fossil fuels. In 2017, for instance, sun and wind produced just 6 percent of the world's electric supply, but they made up 45 percent of the growth in supply, and the cost of sun and wind power continue to fall by about 20 percent with each doubling of capacity. Kingsmill Bond, an English financial analysis, suggests that in the next few years sun and wind power will represent all the growth.[119] We will then reach the peak use of fossil fuels—not because we're running out of them—but because renewable energy will have become so cheap that anyone needing a new energy supply will likely turn to solar or wind power. Bond warned investors that the huge investments in pipelines, tankers, and undersea exploration will be increasingly uncoverable. Precisely how long it will take is impossible to predict, but the outcome seems clear.

The transition is already obvious in the coal market. To understand why Peabody, the world largest private-sector coal-mining company, went from being on Fortune's list of most admired companies in 2008 to bankrupt in 2016 (it emerged from bankruptcy in 2017), let us consider its difficulties in ex-

---

119   Kingsmill Bond. Why you should see the fossil fuel peak coming. Report available at carbon tracker.org.

panding its market. India, until very recently, was expected to provide much of the growth for coal. As late as 2015, its coal use was expected to triple by 2030. But the price of renewable energy began to fall precipitously, and because India suffers from dire air pollution but has inexhaustible supplies of sunlight, its use of solar power increased dramatically. Much of the same is happening around the world. Ironically in 2017, Kentucky's coal mining museum installed solar panels on its roof to save $10,000 a year on electric costs. It is not just coal that is on the way out. Natural gas was supposed to be the planet's next big fuel source, since it produces less carbon dioxide than coal (but its production releases great clouds of methane, another greenhouse gas). But even "cheap" natural gas is starting to look expensive compared to the combination of sun, wind, and batteries.

An original way to collect solar energy comes from our technological progress in genetics. A handful of projects—including an effort by Craig Venter's energy company, Synthetic Genomics—are now underway to use genetically modified photosynthetic organisms to generate fuel with input energy from the sun.

There is no doubt that we are driving on a road that leads to a world without greenhouse gases, the question is whether we can reach that new world in time.

There is also hope on another front: nuclear reactors are going to be safer, cheaper, smaller, and better designed. Developers are hoping to deliver them by the 2020s. Another approach is to resurrect the molten-salt reactor of the 1960s. Its design has been updated with modern technologies and materials that keep the safety features, but lower the cost.[120]

Progress has been made even on nuclear fusion (See

120   *National Geographic*. March 2019, p 32.

appendix 1), which is the great energy hope for humanity. Technical progress is still slow after decades of investment, but fusion companies are focused on containing the plasma required to replicate the thermonuclear conditions of the sun.[121] Though no one expects delivery before 2030, however they bring optimism because they can't melt down and don't create long-lived high level waste. This industry should face much less public resistance than conventional nuclear technology. But many voters simply don't believe companies' promises that new technologies can avoid old mistakes.[122]

California is considering the possibility that its forests could serve as "sinks" for carbon dioxide. One proposal is to reforest previously forested areas. But, a hotter climate could stress existing plant species and harsher droughts could leave these new forests more vulnerable to fire. The hope is that understanding the effects of climate change on California's complex topography and climate zones will help foresters develop the right management strategies, including choosing specific trees that can survive harsh conditions. Unfortunately for the foresters, tree breeding takes a very long time. They will have to resort to genetic engineering if they want to beat the deadline of climate change.

A few years before I was born, my mother went to hear a famous astronomer who was a professor at the College de France.[123] The astronomer finished his lecture by telling the audience: "Look at the telescope. From one side, you can see

---

121   For technical details see Richard Martin's article "Fusion's Future," *MIT Technology Review*, July-August, 2016, p 54.
122   Leigh Phillips. "It Is Time to Reconsider Nuclear Option," *MIT* March-April 2019, p 46.
123   The College de France is a public higher education ad research institution in France and has no equivalent abroad. To be a professor there is a high honor.

the universe, but if you look from the other side (outside in) you will see man's brain, a fantastic tool to interpret the universe. Today let use our brain to solve the problem of pollution and climate change."

This solution will come from the brains of scientists so long as they are given time and the means. I already mentioned that some of them are working on artificial photosynthesis (artificial trees), which would permit to capture carbon dioxide.[124] There may yet still be undiscovered ways to solve the problem of the greenhouse effect before it is too late. Scientists should have the freedom to explore and a few billion dollars. We spent billions of dollars going to the moon. Surely we can spend a few more to save us from a sure catastrophe.

Today many are conscious of the dangers proposed by pollution and climate change, but there is far less concern about the danger of nuclear weapons. Since 1945, we have lived under radioactive clouds that are ready to break at any moment. Except for nuclear physicists, no one is talking about the terrible dangers nuclear explosions pose, which makes it harder to be optimistic about solving the problem of nuclear war.

---

124   I read this somewhere, but I cannot remember where.

8

Mankind Must Unite or Perish

We need to hold out our vision of a different world, in which national borders are erased and we are truly one human family in which we treat children all over the world as our children, which means we could never engage in war.

Howard Zinn [125]

We must prevent nuclear wars. Treaties calling for an abandonment of nuclear weapons have been signed, but nations continue to build more deadly options. And abolishing nuclear weapons today would not prevent nations from building them again in the future. The world must make a conscious decision to stop killing each other for stupid reasons. This is the only choice because nuclear war is suicidal. Thermal radiation will be so intense that no one will survive.

The only hope for peace and survival is to create a global government that prevents wars. The reader may think I am completely crazy to propose such a solution to preventing

---

125   Zinn, Howard. *Howard Zinn Speaks: Collected Speeches 1963-2009.* (Chicago, Haymarket Books, 2012), p 204.

nuclear war, because we are in a time of a resurgence of nationalism in Britain, Russia, the United States, China, and other countries. I know the world is not ready to unite, but the creation of nuclear weapons has left us no other choice.

I am not the only idealist who dreams of outlawing war. Many know at least a fair amount about The League of Nations and The United Nations, but few know or remember that sixty-three nations signed the Paris Peace Pact (known in the United States as The Kellogg-Brian Pact) in 1928 to outlaw war. Those who signed the Pact sought to end war between states by renouncing war as an instrument of national policy.

One does not have to be an historian to know that the Paris Peace Pact failed to end wars. In 1931, Japan invaded China. In 1935, Italy invaded Ethiopia. In 1939, Germany invaded Poland and then most of Europe. Twenty-one years after World War I, the world was again involved in another war far more destructive than the one that preceded it.

The death toll of the Second World War (combatants and civilians) was five times that of the First World War—an unimaginable seventy million people died.[126] The Paris Peace Pact did not stop the wars that followed, but it was the first step of an idealistic ladder leading to global peace. It abandoned the Old World Order—the legal regime that European States adopted in the seventeenth century (with the treaties of Westphalia). The rules that defined the Old World Order differed starkly from those that govern today. They were not against waging war. They were about waging war in the right way. They were understood to be obligatory, and sovereigns largely obeyed them. Before 1928, every state accepted the position that war was not a departure from civilized politics,

---

126   Milton Leitenberg. *Deaths in Wars and Conflicts in the 20th Century*, 2003.

it was civilized politics. War was simply accepted as the con-
tinuation of politics by other means.[127] It was an instrument
of justice. To murder is morally monstrous and obviously
criminal. But somehow, when slaughter takes place after a
formal declaration of war, it suddenly becomes legal. Even
stranger, soldiers did not merely have the license to kill in
war, they also have the license to trespass, destroy property,
commit arson, and maim and rape women. In other words,
they have a license to perform acts that would constitute
criminality if committed in peace time.

After 1928, war was outlawed, at least in principle. States
no longer had the right to conquer others states. Gunboat diplomacy was no longer legitimate. On the other hand, economic sanctions became a way in which international law
could be enforced. In this "New World Order" wars are un-
controversial, yet rarely bring anything positive. Some wars
may be just, such as repelling military aggression or preventing humanitarian disasters, but diplomacy should always
play a role before turning to war.

The emissaries who signed the Peace Pact in 1928 had
no inkling of the chaos they would unleash. Their goal of
outlawing war was glorious, yet, little did they realize it was
also perilous. They removed the linchpin of the international
system. By eliminating war as a tool for solving international
disputes, they left the remaining rules of the system suspend-
ed and it did not take long for the international legal order to
fall to pieces.

According to Dona Hathaway and Scott Shapiro, law
professors at Yale University, the Pact was naïve, but not for
the reason most think.

---

127   Carl Von Clausewitz. *On War* (Princeton: Princeton University Press, 1976), p 87.

Outlawing war did work. If anything, it worked too well. The problem with the Peace Pact was that it was purely destructive. By outlawing war, states renounced the principal means they had for resolving their disputes. They demolished the existing system, which had allowed states to right wrongs with force, but they failed to replace it with a new system. This was in part because there was already an institution—the League of Nations—that seemed poised to resolve disputes. But the League was built on Old World Order principles. It, too, relied on war and the threat of war to right wrongs and to enforce the rules. In a world in which war was outlawed, however, the League's enforcement mechanism was grounded in a power that states were reluctant to yield.[128]

As the world hurtled toward disaster in the 1930s, philosophers, layers, and statesmen struggled to answer the question of how to fill the vacuum left by the outlawing of war. Their failure to achieve a consensus as to how to respond to illegal behavior—if not with war—created chaos and paralysis, thwarting the possibility of a coordinated and thus effective response to the Axis threat.

The League of Nations

Our ancestors did not develop a concern for human race's survival until the end of World War I when they created the League of Nations and declared that this war [World War 1] was the "last war." The idea of an institution entrusted with

---

128   Oona Hathway and Scott Shapiro. *The Internationalists* (New York: Simon and Schuster, 2017), p XVI.

preventing wars was marvelous, but, unfortunately, only a dream. The League of Nations failed in its mission for many reasons, but mainly because it took its instruction from national authorities whose concern was overwhelmingly for their own interest and advantage. To succeed, institutions like the League of Nations must consider world values over local and national values.

The task of the League of Nations' was simple—to ensure that war never broke again. After the slaughter and political turmoil caused by the Versailles treaty,[129] many looked to the League to bring stability to the world. If another dispute did occur, the League, under its covenant, could do three things known as the sanctions:

It could call on the states in dispute to sit down and discuss the problem in an orderly and peaceful manner. This would be done in the League's Assembly, which would listen to disputes and come to a decision on how to proceed.

If one nation was seen to be the offender, the League would warn the aggressing nation that she would need to leave the other nation's territory or face the consequences. If the states in dispute failed to listen to the Assembly's decision, the League could introduce economic sanctions. The purpose of this sanction was to financially hit the aggressing nation so that she would have to do as the League required. The logic behind it was to push an aggressor nation towards bankruptcy. The League could order its members not to do any trade with an aggressor nation to bring peace.

If this failed, the League could introduce physical sanc-

---

129 The Treaty of Versailles became the first treaty in America's history that the Senate did not ratify. Without America's participation, the League soon showed its impotence in the face of territorial aggression by Japan and Italy and fell into abeyance.

tions. This meant military force would be used to put into place the League's decision. However, the League did not have a military force at its disposal and no member of the League had to provide one. Therefore, the League could not carry any threats and any country defying its authority would have been very aware of this weakness. The League had other weaknesses.

America's president at the time, Woodrow Wilson, had dreamed up the League but refused to join it. Germany wasn't allowed to join the League because she had started the war; hence, she could not be part of the international community. Russia was not allowed to join either, because it had a communist government that generated fear in Western Europe. These three nations played no part in supporting the League.

The League of Nations had some successes. One of them concerned the Åland Islands that are nearly equal distant between Finland and Sweden. They had traditionally belonged to Finland, but most of the Islanders wanted to be governed by Sweden. Neither Sweden nor Finland could come to a decision as to who owned the islands and in 1921 they asked the League to adjudicate. The League's decision was that the islands should remain with Finland but that no weapons should be ever kept. Both countries accepted the decision and it remains enforced to this day.

Another success was in Upper Silesia. The Treaty of Versailles had given the people of Upper Silesia the right to have a referendum on whether they wanted to be part of Germany or Poland. In this referendum, 700,000 voted for Germany and 500,000 for Poland. This "close" vote resulted in rioting and The League was asked to settle this dispute. After a six-week inquiry, it decided to split Upper Silesia between Germany and Poland. The League decision was accepted by both countries and by the people in Upper Silesia.

If the League of Nations had some successes, it also had capital failures. It failed to act against Japan's aggression in China in 1931; take effective measures against Italy's aggression in Africa in 1935; respond to the unilateral German denunciation of the Treaty of Versailles and notably its military reoccupation of the Rhineland in 1936; nor to respond to the Nazi occupation of Austria and then Czechoslovakia.

In 1919, Italian nationalists were angered because they believed that the "Big Three" had broken promises at the Treat of Versailles by giving the port of Fiume to Yugoslavia. On September 12, 1919, an Italian nationalist, Gabriele D'Annunzio,[130] exploited a dispute between the Kingdoms of Serbs, Croats, and Slovenes (later the kingdom of Yugoslavia) and entered the city with his own troops to govern Fiume for 15 months. The situation was solved by the Italian government who could not accept that D'Annunzio was seemingly more popular than they were—so they bombarded the port of Fiume and forced him to surrender. Fiume then became an independent state. The League played no part in this dispute even though its sole purpose was to maintain peace.

Another example, was the town of Vilna. Historically, Vilna was the capital of Lithuania when the state existed in the Middle Ages. But after World War I, Lithuania was reestablished and Vilna was the natural choice for its capital. However, by 1930, 30 percent of the population was Polish with Lithuanians only making up 2 percent of the city's population. In 1920, the Poles seized Vilna. Lithuania asked for League's help, but the Poles could not be persuaded to leave the city. Vilna stayed in Polish hands until the outbreak of World War II. The Polish's use of force allowed them to win.

Also in 1920, Poland invaded land held by the Russians.

---

130   Gabriele D'Annunzio was a famous writer, poet, journalist.

The Poles quickly overwhelmed the Russian army and made a swift advance into Russia. By 1921, the Russians had no choice but to sign the Treaty of Riga which handed over nearly 800,000 square kilometers of Russian land to Poland. This one treaty doubled the size of Poland. What did the League do about this violation of another country by Poland? The answer is simple—nothing. By 1919 Russia was a communist country and this plague from the East was greatly feared by the West. In fact, Britain, France, and America sent troops to attack Russia after the League of Nations had been set up. Winston Churchill, the British War Minister, stated openly that plan was to strangle Communist Russia at birth. Once again, to outsiders, it seemed as if the League was selecting which countries were acceptable and which ones were not. The Allied invasion was a total failure and only served to make Communist Russia even more antagonistic to the West.

The Treaty of Versailles had ordered Germany to pay reparations for war damages. These could either be paid in money or in kind (goods to the value of a set amount). In 1922, the Germans failed to pay an installment, claiming they simply could not afford it. The Allies refused to accept this excuse. Both the French and Belgian governments believed that some form of strong action was needed to "teach Germany a lesson." So, in 1923, contrary to League rules, the French and the Belgians invaded the Ruhr—Germany's most important industrial zone. France was a senior League member breaking rules and nothing was done about it. It became obvious to other nations that breaking League rules wasn't hard to do.

This was the beginning of the end of the League of Nations.

This breakdown encouraged Fascist Italy to align itself with Nazi Germany, a crisis that brought an end to peace in

Europe. It was clear by 1937 there were two definite sides on the European continent. This leads to the biggest failure of the League of Nations: its inability to prevent World War II.

In brief, the League of Nations was formed with the aim of preventing another appalling conflict such as World War I. This aim failed leading to weakened states, economic depression, renewed European nationalism, and the rise of Nazism due to German humiliation. These conditions eventually led to World War II, which was far worse than World War I in destruction and death of both soldiers and civilians. Would the next attempt to prevent war, the United Nations (UN), be more successful?

The United Nations

The Atlantic Charter, which was announced in a joint statement on August 14, 1941, set a sure course for the Allies, bound America and Britain together in a set of inspirational war aims, and began to hint at the new world organizations that would regulate the postwar world. The earliest concrete plan for a new world organization to replace the ineffective League of Nations began under the aegis of the U.S. Department in 1939. Its name was suggested by President Roosevelt to British Prime Minister Winston Churchill during the latter's three-week visit to the White House in December 1941.

The text of the Declaration by the United Nations was drafted by President Roosevelt, Winston Churchill, and Roosevelt's aide Harry Hopkins at the White House on December 29. It incorporated Soviet suggestions. Over January 1-2 1942, twenty-six governments signed the Declaration. By early 1945, it had been signed by 21 more states. During the war, the United Nations became the official term for the Allies. To join, countries had to sign the Declaration and declare war on the Axis (Germany, Italy, and Japan). The United Nations became an international organization in declarations signed at the wartime Allied conferences: the Moscow conference and the Tehran conference in 1943. The name 'United Nations' was adopted during the 1945 United Nations Conference on International Organization in San Francisco where they also drafted the UN Charter.

The founders of the United Nations had a clear vision of its roles and responsibilities. It would act as a facilitator of cooperative action among sovereign nations to prevent repetition of the twin scourges of global conflict and economic depression. The 1945 Charter of the United Nations established four purposes for the organization:

1   To maintain international peace and security, and to that end: to take effective collective measures for the prevention and removal of threats to the peace.

2   To develop friendly relations among nations based on respect for the principle of equal rights and self-determination of peoples.

3   To achieve international cooperation in solving international problems of an economic, social, cultural, or humanitarian character, and in promoting and encouraging respect for human rights and for fundamental freedoms.

4   To be a center for harmonizing the actions of nations in the attainment of these common ends.[131]

The United Nations Security Council (UNSC) is one of the five principal organs of the United Nations. Its purpose

---

131   Charter of the United Nations part 1, parts 1-4.

is to maintain international peace and security as well as accept new members to the United Nations and approve any changes to the United Nations charter. Its power includes the establishment of peace keeping operations, international sanctions, and the authorization of military action through Security Council resolutions. These were developed by then Secretary-General, Dag Hammarskjöld and Canadian diplomat, Leslie Pearson in response to the botched Anglo-French Israeli invasion of Egypt in 1956. It is the only UN body with the authority to issue binding resolutions to member states.

The Security Council consists of fifteen members. The body's five permanent members are the victors of World War Two: The Soviet Union (now represented by Russia), Great Britain, France, China (now represented by the People's Republic of China), and the United States. These permanent members can veto any substantive Security Council resolution, including those on the admission of new member states or candidates for Secretary General. The Security Council has also ten non-permanent members, elected on a regional basis to serve two-year terms. The body's presidency rotates monthly about its members.

To understand the weakness of the United Nations one should remember that the international organization is not an international legislature that passes laws binding all the people of the World. The UN Charter is not a global constitution. The Security Council is a political, not judicial body. The International Court of Justice, or World Court, is best understood as an arbitral panel with a limited jurisdiction and no actual enforcement authority.

In its early decades, the Security Council was largely paralyzed by the Cold War division between the US and USSR and their respective allies, though it authorized interventions in Korea, the Congo, Cyprus, and West New Guinea. When the cold war ended it seemed for a while as if the United Nations might at last be able to work as its founders had originally intended. But the nature of peace and war as well as the other challenges facing the organization were different from what governments thought they were facing in 1945 when the charter was written. The bloody conflicts that the public assumed should be the responsibility of the United Nations—Yugoslavia, Somalia, Cambodia, and East Timor, for instance—were more frequently within the borders of a single state than between states and it was not the job of the United Nations to intervene.

With the collapse of the Soviet Union, UN peacekeeping efforts increased dramatically in scale, and the Security Council authorized major military and peacekeeping missions in Kuwait, Namibia, Cambodia, Bosnia, Sudan, and the Democratic Republic of Congo. In 1986, there were five operations with 10,000 uniformed personnel and a budget of $240 million. In contrast, in 1993, at the height of UN involvement in the Balkans, there were fifteen operations with 55,000 uniformed personnel and a budget of $2.7 billion.[132]

These missions were not only larger but also of a different character than those of the cold war era. Instead of being on the borders separating the military forces of one nation from another, after or at least at the end of a conflict, UN peace-keepers were largely deployed inside countries, in many cases while fighting still raged. They either had an explicit mandate from the Security Council to deal with the political, human rights, and humanitarian issues; or they found

---

132   Jean Mary Guehenno. *The Fog of Peace: A Memoir of International Peacekeeping in the twenty-first century* (Brookings Institution Press, 2015).

that, even without a mandate, they were obliged to deal with these issues.

The late 1990s marked the nadir of the reputation of the UN's peacekeeping missions. They could not avert the massacre of thousands of civilians by Serbian and other forces in the former Yugoslavia. The conflict in Yugoslavia (the Kosovo War) was ended by the intervention NATO forces, justifying its intervention as a humanitarian war and in act taking the role of the UN. The NATO bombing campaign has remained controversial, as it did not get the approval of the UN Security Council and because it caused deaths of Yugoslav civilians. The UN was also unable to intervene in Rwanda in time to stop or even curtail the genocide that went on between 1991 and 1995.

Why so many failures on the part of the United Nations to keep peace? Too many mandates were unachievable because they demanded far more robust forces that the United Nations could find. There was an overstretching of UN peacekeeping. For example, in 2004, the Security Council expanded the mission in the Democratic Republic of Congo, while deploying new missions in Haiti and Cote d'Ivoire.

According to Jean Marie Guehenno, the former undersecretary general for peacekeeping operations, by the time of the United States' invasion of Iraq the UN was an organization under siege from many of its member states, especially the US. He notes, "the most painful lesson of Iraq was actually how little care, political as well as human, key member states showed for the organization they had created in 1945."[133] Most flagrantly, the US and UK disregarded the findings of UN inspector Hans Blix, that no weapons of mass destruction had been found in Iraq and that the search for them should

---

133   Ibid.

continue. We now know that there were none and that the war with all its causalities was useless—as most wars are. Now, the Middle East is in flames. Destruction is total.

There have been a lot of criticisms of the United Nations, particularly of the Security Council, which has been described as an undemocratic international body. Many argue it fails its principal task mainly because of the veto power of its permanent members. They might be right when the US routinely uses its veto to protect Israel from criticism of its abuses committed in the occupied Palestinian territories and when Russia uses its veto to obstruct any significant effort in addressing the Syrian slaughter since peaceful protests began in March 2011.

There are other weaknesses with the nature of the United Nations. For example, the UN mandate to promote and protect human rights was the result of a political compromise to resolve two competing principles: promotion and protection of human rights and the sovereign right of non-intervention into a nation's internal affairs.[134] While not inherently conflicting, these two principles come into conflict frequently. Because of this disagreement, the UN Charter provides for only a limited mandate to protect rights, compared to the Charter's mandate to protect international peace and security. In other words, the United Nations cannot remove dictators who have no respect for human rights or the treatment of minorities.[135] Ideally, any new international government

---

134   Article II, part 7 reads, "Nothing contained in the present Charter shall authorize the United Nations to intervene in matters which are essentially within the domestic jurisdiction of any state."
135   The refusal in 2003 of the Security Council to authorize the disastrous US war on Iraq thus saved the UN from possibly terminal discredit in the eyes of much of the rest of the world.

must have this power. I say "ideally" because it might be impossible to accomplish this as long as separate nations exist.

Another weakness affecting the efficacy of the United Nations is that the UN has never had a standing army ready to carry out the directives of the Security Council. It has instead engaged, with varying success in different kinds of "peace keeping," using forces recruited by the UN secretariat. UN peacekeepers are military forces provided by member states and funded independently of the main UN budget. Today, a UN contingent is more likely to be provided by poor countries from Africa or Asia, eager for UN cash. These soldiers are inexperienced, undisciplined, and not always well-regarded by those whose peace they have to keep.[136] Additionally, a fresh contingent has to be raised for each crisis. *This is an argument for the United Nations or a future international organization to have its own permanent army.*

Virtually unknown in 1945, the world is facing global problems today that no government can successfully deal with by itself. They include nuclear proliferation, the deterioration of the environment, global warming, international terrorism, and a probable future shortage of such necessities as clean water. As a universal organization, the United Nations should be uniquely suited to provide leadership and coordination of action on such matters. But the capacity of its members has been limited and disappointing, as was recently shown at the Copenhagen and Paris meetings on climate change. Some important groups object, in principle as well as in practice, to independent international organizations, and especially to an active, international secretariat.

Since 1945, scarcely a year has gone by without the sub-

---

136   Tony Judt. *When the Facts change.* (London: William Heinemann, 2015), p 259.

ject of UN reform surfacing in one way or another. From time to time useful reforms, mostly in organization and in the Secretariat, have been made. The attitudes and responsibilities of the governments involved in the organization have seldom if ever been touched on.

Thomas Weiss, professor of political science at the CUNY Graduate Center and director of the Ralph Bunch Institute for International Studies, discussed in his scholarly book, *What's Wrong with The United Nations and How to Fix It*,[137] the probable and eventual need for some world government, a subject regarded as a dangerous heresy in the Congress of the United States. Weiss points out that although the UN's original purpose was to protect member nations against external aggression, sovereignty and power remain vested in those nations. Since the UN's founding, the need for international management both of political crisis and of global problems has steadily grown, while the incidence of wars between nations has steadily decreased. "Treating traditional sovereignty as a cornerstone for the United Nations," Weiss declares, "is a fundamental structural weakness in urgent need of replacement." Weiss is right because the concept of sovereignty, established by the Treaty of Westphalia in 1648 is too old and inadequate today. He compared that concept to a virus that renders the UN unable to protect humanity from solving global problems. It is time to abandon the concept of national sovereignty, and adopt a post Westphalian international order.

The UN secretariat, an easy target, is also in continual and urgent need of reform. In a chapter entitled: "Overwhelming Bureaucracy and Underwhelming Leadership,"

---

137   Thomas Weiss. *What's Wrong with the United Nations and How to Fix It?*

Weiss denounces the UN's tendency to appoint senior officials for political reasons rather than for their competence
and qualifications. In theory, at least, the secretary general is
the only UN official selected by governments. The vital ap-
pointment has always been a political lottery controlled by
the five permanent members of the Security Council, which
selects a candidate for the approval of the General Assembly.
Candidates now conduct worldwide election campaigns,
which means that the council devotes little attention or effort
to searching for the best possible man or woman for the job;
the main preoccupation is often to find a noncontroversial
candidate who will not be vetoed by any of the permanent
members. It is largely a matter of luck whether the person
appointed can do a good, or even an adequate job, in an ex-
traordinarily demanding office. Correcting this situation is
the indispensable first step in any serious reform of the Secretariat, not to mention for ensuring the quality of the leadership of the organization as a whole.

Events have occasionally driven the UN to adopt new
principles. The horror of the Rwandan genocide, for instance,
impelled Secretary General, Kofi Annan to put forward the
concept of "responsibility to protect," which, after being cau-
tiously approved by a summit meeting of heads of state in
2005, opened a possible door for the international rescue of
groups in unbearable misery or under lethal harassment in
their own country. Peacekeeping, an improvisation not mentioned in the UN Charter is now universally accepted. At any
given moment more than 100,000 peacekeeping soldiers are
on duty in many parts of the world. No progress has been
made toward a standing UN rapid deployment force, which,
in an ideal world, would be the obvious way to provide the
speedy deployment of well-trained troops in an emergency.

In discussions on UN reforms, government representatives tend to avoid mentioning this debilitating powerlessness. Weiss makes a stirring argument for dropping the current coyness about steps that might lead to a world government in the distant future and for starting to discuss seriously what is needed to establish a stable, peaceful, and unthreatened international society in an age of potentially terminal global problems.

In his book, Weiss is not interested in tinkering with the UN—his proposals are bold and far reaching. Drawing on his own experience within the UN system (he has held several UN positions) and studying it from outside, Weiss clears away a lot of the debris of superficial critiques to uncover the deeper explanations for why the more world problems become interconnected and global in scope, the less the UN seems to be able to cope with them.

Ban Ki-moon, who was the eighth UN Secretary General, said in an interview with Elizabeth Dias that:

When member states are divided, the UN cannot function properly. When Security Council members are united, they have been able to address the issues protecting international peace and security. I'm concerned about the growing trend of nationalism in many parts of the world. We are living on, after all, a very small planet. There is not much meaning at this time to the geographic borders of individual national regulations. We are going through a rapid, transformational process of globalization that we have to act as a human being. We have to act as a global citizen.[138]

Mention of the UN in the US, especially in Washington,

---

138   Elizabeth Diaz, Ban Li-moon. *Time* Jan 2, 2017, p 70.

and you will likely hear that it is a "scandal," "waste," and failure." It is seen as an expensive international excrescence, a breeding ground for inertia, sinecures, and timeservers, an impediment to the efficient pursuit and prosecution of American national interest. In these circles, the UN is at best a good idea gone "wrong."

Although the UN failed to prevent war, it was successful elsewhere. We should be reminded of the astonishing reach of the UN through its various agencies in the fields of population, environment, agriculture, development, education, medicine, refugee care, and much else. The United Nations addresses humanitarian crises and challenges that most people in the Western World cannot begin to imagine. The UN works best when everyone acknowledges the legitimacy of its role, for example, when monitoring or overseeing elections or truces, or when intervening in the fight against a viral disease such as Ebola.[139]

Although I am not an historian or a political scientist, it seems to me that there are (and were) flagrant missteps in the structures of both the League of Nations and the United Nations whose aims were to prevent war. They failed in great part because some nations had veto powers and there was no real international army to enforce the decisions of either organization. To have peace, we need all the nations to unite. Whether we like it or not, the invention of nuclear weapons is forcing us to consider a strong global world government that should have its own army to enforce the rules and prevent any war. If we had such an army we would have prevented the disaster in the Middle East and other parts of the world.

In any case, the choice is ours. If we unite we might be

---

139   Paul Kennedy. *The Parliament of Man: The Past, Present and Future of the United Nations* (New York: Random House, 2006).

able to solve the deadly problems that face us. If we do not, chances are that we will disappear, but the moon will continue to go around the earth, the sun will continue to be bright, and the universe will continue to expand.

The Lack of Scientific Literacy

After witnessing the horror brought on by one of science's major achievements (the atomic bomb) in World War II, many scientists believed in educating the public on the fact that science could be used not only for good, but also for evil. They sought civilian control of nuclear energy. Thus, was born a loosely structured, but high visible movement that came to be called "scientific literacy."

A number of scientific organizations and public interest groups were formed in 1945, notably among these being the Federation of Scientists and the Federation of Atomic Scientists. In 1946, the Chicago chapter of the Federation of American Scientists began publishing the *Bulletin of Atomic Scientists* (which later became an independent journal and a highly regarded publication). The common belief was that the science and technology of the atomic bomb had brought civilization to the edge of a precipice, and that civilization may very well push itself over the edge due to a lack of reasonable decision-making processes when it came to using such destructive technologies.

Educating the public failed because while most students (and adults) may find science interesting, they also find it difficult and unrewarding to learn. At the end of the nineteenth century, T.H. Huxley sought to persuade the public that science was not a form of black art but rather a kind of common sense. He argued that both scientists and the public use inductive and deductive reasoning in their everyday activities.[140] "Thus," he said, "one should not conclude that science has a special way of looking at things that is not also the way of ordinary people except that scientists must be somewhat more precise and take greater care in verifying their conclusions through appropriate experiments."

He was partially correct then, but would be less so today. The fact is that modern science, mathematics (especially physics), and the kind of reasoning that is characteristic of science are remote from one's everyday experience. The universe could still be commonly described as well-behaved and deterministic until the end of the 19th century. But the picture changed at the beginning of the 20th century, when science's most basic concepts became so abstract that they defied common understanding. To make matters worse, the public began to view the universe as a "cosmic game of chance." (See appendix 2). We lost not only the public, but scientists who were not physicists. It is understandable that most people do not comprehend modern physics: It takes a lot of imagination to do so.

But, we do not need a complete understanding of the quantum theory or general relativity to invent modern products and instruments that result from basic research. Modern mediums of communication operate through the transmission of electromagnetic waves, whose existence was predicted by Maxwell and confirmed experimentally by Hertz. Induction coils on automobiles observe Faraday's law of in-

---

140   T.H. Huxley. *"We Are All Scientists" in Darwinian* (New York: Appleton Century, 1863).

duction. Nuclear power was made possible by the discovery
and splitting of the atomic nucleus by Rutherford, Fermi, the
Curies, and others. Basic circuits used in computers were discovered by nuclear physicists in the 1930s. Transistors were
invented by physicists doing quantum mechanical research
into solids. The laser, the vacuum tube, the Josepshon junc-
tion, and the superconducting magnet were all invented from
the course of basic research.

But the lack of scientific knowledge among the public ex-
tends beyond physics, and to biology. In the 21st century there
are still people who do not know the difference between a
virus and a bacterium. Parents ask for antibiotics to combat
a viral infection. Antibiotics kill bacteria but not viruses. A
physician friend of mine told me that it was easier to give
children sugar pills than to explain to their parents the nature
of viruses. Surveys have consistently shown the desperately
poor state of scientific literacy in the United States.

Most science teachers in high school or college give ex-
ams that are focused on facts and require students to apply
formulae that express natural laws. Today's knowledge is
still dogmatically presented as the ultimate truth, which is a
mistake. Besides being static, it gives rise to the false impression that science is absolute and unchangeable—that the only
road to progress is drawing the consequence of forever-true
principles. Such erroneous ideas destroy much of the educa-
tional value of teaching science.

One such idea is that there is such a thing as the scientific
method, as James Conant, one of the best-known American
scientists and former president of Harvard University, says
in one of his famous lectures:

It would be my thesis that those historians of science,
and I might add philosophers as well, who emphasize

that there is no such thing as the scientific method are doing a public service. To my mind, some of the oversimplified accounts of science and its working to be found in the elementary texts in high schools, for example, are based on a fallacious reading of the history of physics, chemistry and biology.[141].

To become a famous scientist, you need more than the scientific method: you need imagination and a fearlessness in contradicting the knowledge of your time.

For many years, science has been included among the areas of study that make up a liberal education at the undergraduate level. It seems to have been agreed that some exposure to science was desirable, as were introductory surveys in literature, philosophy, and a range of other subjects. But what types of courses should be taught to non-science majors? For prospective scientists and engineers, the introductory science courses have usually been demanding and rigorous. They cannot be used for non-science majors. And so many science departments offer elementary courses specifically aimed at liberal arts majors. These courses tend to be highly qualitative, and often use a bare minimum of mathematics. Their objective is to explain the observed phenomena of the world in simple terms. Physics is easier to dilute for a standard freshman course, but it still requires many homework problems that are not appreciated by non-science students. The overwhelming impression that one gains is that these courses dare not to be too demanding for fear of failing too many students, and that even this sort of exposure to science will serve some broad "purpose." Enrollment in

---

141   James Conant. *Modern Science and Modern Man* (New York: A Doubleday Anchor Book, 1953) p 35.

many of these courses is maintained only because of a science requirement. Unfortunately, these survey courses have been seen as "something to get out of the way," perhaps even mercifully during a summer session.

For years Michigan State University had a college whose function was to teach general education in humanities, social sciences, and natural sciences. I was in the department of natural science from 1965 to 1989. Since my retirement I have wondered if we were successful. I concluded that little was accomplished. Sure, students who were not science majors, might have learned some facts about science, but not the nature of science despite all our efforts.

According to my students, I gave the best lecture at the end of my teaching career in which I told them that I failed to discover that the chromosome of a virus was a circle, not a straight line like those of fruit flies and humans. A few years later someone else came up with the idea. That day my students learn that successful scientists use 1 percent inspiration and 99 percent perspiration. They learned how much of research is trial and error and how much depends on factors other than scientific laws and methods. As a matter of fact, scientists do not spend much of their time thinking about scientific laws at all. They are busy with other things, such as getting some apparatus to work, finding a way to measure something more exactly, or trying to find a solution to a problem that might come up at 3:00 a.m. one day.

I told my students that the scientific road to knowledge is not smooth but rocky with many detours, and that scientists seldom follow the shortest road from one discovery to another; it is only retrospectively that the real direction of man's endeavor can be distinguished among all ways in which they squandered time and energy. Many of the false moves are, of course, not recorded, but some have been, and should be known. For instance, Thomas Morgan, a distinguished geneticist at Columbia University in the beginning of the twentieth century, published a hypothesis explaining the inheritance of certain traits associated with sex in the fruit fly, but had to discard it a year later because of more intensive experimentation. He came up with another hypothesis for which he received the Nobel Prize. Other examples can be given in biology and other fields of science.

The public generally has no idea how scientific discoveries are made. They believe that given enough money, scientists will discover the cause of cancer. Sure, money helps, but they also need imagination and a prepared mind, like Louis Pasteur once said, "Sometimes luck plays a role." In 1896, the physicist Henri Becquerel, accidentally left a piece of uranium on a photographic plate while experimenting on X-rays, upon being developed, the plate was shown to have been bombarded by a powerful radiation coming from within the uranium. This new type of emission was christened as radioactivity. Another famous example was when Alexander Fleming, a Scottish bacteriologist, returned from a two-week vacation to find that mold had accidentally contaminated a staphylococcus culture plate. The mold seems to have prevented the growth of the bacterium, staphylococcus. This led to the beginning of antibiotics. Another lesser known example is the discovery that seeds of some trees need heat (approximately 60 degrees C) to germinate. A future PhD had left the seeds on a Petri dish in a small oven. Someone had turned it on during the night and the seeds germinated. This explained why those tree species are the first to reappear after forest fires.

I do not believe that luck will help us stop the effects of climate change, but it is possible that someone is going to

come up with a fantastic and practical idea to do it and succeed with the help of everyone else.

Certain science television programs such as PBS's, *Nature,*
do not help the public's confusion when they give teleogical
explanations for the existence of an animal or plant charac-
teristics. Teleology consists of explanations in terms of end
purposes or functions. Modern biologists usually use it to
make the end preexistent as an efficient cause and to require
consciousness on the part of the purposeful agent. Thus, in
explaining various animal organs to students, it is custom-
ary to cite their function or purpose; for example, birds have
wings to fly. This is a not a good explanation because some
birds that have wings cannot fly. The ancestors of birds were
not as well adapted to fly as they are today. One could ask
why some species of birds fly better than others? Why are
birds in the first place? Is flying natural? After all there were
flying dinosaurs. Evolution is part of life, but understanding
how organisms evolve requires an understanding of genetics
and natural selection. This knowledge is not common, and it
is easier to give a teleogical explanation because most people will accept it. For example, humans developed hands to
better grasp tools, or animals developed limbs so they could
navigate on land. Maybe evolution is what is hard to grasp!
People have heard of Charles Darwin and his theory of natural selection, but are confused about its meaning. Natural
selection plays a role among individuals of the same species,
not between species.

Since the 2016 U.S. national elections there have been
attempts to silence science. Journalists and whistle-blowers
have exposed some alarming moves by federal and state governments to restrict science research, education, and commu-

nication.[142] Tactics run the gamut from censorship and funding cuts to destroying data, twisting studies, and removing scientists from advisory boards. It appears we are back in time, one hundred years ago, when teachers could not teach evolution. Are we going to push back against these scientific abuses by voting in more scientifically-minded congress people, and for a president who takes seriously the dangers that menace us?

In brief, why is it so difficult for people to understand that the next global war might be the last if nuclear weapons are used? I believe it is because they know very little about science and technology, which they confuse one for the other. They blame science when they should blame technology. Technology is the application of what scientists have discovered. Science is a branch of knowledge. Technology is applied science. In the chapter about the atomic bomb I said that those who first discovered the immense energy inside an atom had a very good idea of its uses for either good or evil. This is true for anyone who invents anything—he or she can never be certain that the invention will not have some harmful consequences. The automobile increased individual mobility and hence personal freedom. But in addition to taking on its own death toll, it was a prime cause of suburban sprawl, inner city decay, and air pollution. Nuclear power provides energy, but it can also bring a nuclear holocaust.

142   Mark Fischetti. "Silencing Science," *Scientific American*, May 2019, p 88.

Conclusion

The indictment of war is that the purposes served can never justify the costs. While instances might be found to refute this charge attempts to defend war as a mean of resolving disputes have struggled since the arrival of nuclear weapons in 1945. The possibility that they could be employed in a Third World War created a catastrophic prospect, and not only for the belligerents, but also for humanity as a whole, and the confusion and discord would reach unimaginable levels. This is one reason why the major powers held back from another great war, even as they kept their military inventories and conducted research into new generations of weaponry. Without much difficulty, they looked into the likely character of a future war and decided that this war as not one they could survive.

Lawrence Freedman

More than fifty years ago Rachel Carlson wrote *Silent Spring*, a book that was a devastating attack on human carelessness, greed, and irresponsibility. She blames us for having contaminated the air, earth, rivers, and sea with dangerous and even lethal materials. She makes a parallel between this type of contamination and radiation released through nuclear explosions. In both cases pollution is irrevocable. For example, strontium 90, a radioactive isotope produced by nuclear fission with a half-life of 28.8 years, comes to earth in rain or drifts down as fallout, lodges in soil, enters plants, and in time takes up its abode in the bones of human beings until their untimely death. Carlson warns us:

> Chemicals sprayed on croplands or forests or gardens lie long in soil, entering into living organisms, passing from one to another in a chain of poisoning and death. Or they pass mysteriously by underground streams until they emerge and, through the alchemy of air and sunlight, combine into new forms that kill vegetation, sicken cattle, and work unknown harm on those who drink from once pure wells.[143]

Carlson also warns us that we have spoiled the Earth so fast that life is threatened because organisms cannot adapt to the new environment.

> The chemicals to which life is asked to make its adjustment are no longer merely the calcium and silica and copper and all the rest of the minerals washed out of the rocks and carried in rivers to the sea; they are the synthetic creations of man's inventive mind, brewed in his laboratories, and having no counterparts in nature.[144]

Fifty years after she wrote *Silent Spring*, little has changed,

---

143   Rachel Carlson. *Silent Spring*. (New York: Fawcett Crest Book, April 1970) 16-17.
144   Ibid.

birds came back, but pollution is still here and more intense than before. We have polluted not only the Earth, but also space.

We are faced with two other great dangers: climate change and nuclear war. Although scientists have known for many years that the Earth has been warming up, it is only in the last decade that the pubic have too realized the danger of climate change. The effects are all around us: heat waves, storms, hurricanes, melting glaciers, droughts, floods, and rising sea levels. Solving this problem requires a total revolution in our way of life. We must sacrifice convenience to forestall the penalty imposed on future generations. We need complete cooperation between nations, which at the present, is far from forthcoming.

Although the danger of nuclear war is not ignored, its gravity is not understood by most people. Two atomic bombs were used end World War II in 1945, but have never been used since. People are afraid of nuclear weapons because they are deadly. The logical answer is DON'T USE THEM! GET RID OF THEM! But so far, every nation is fearful of what will happen if it does not have nuclear weapons. Denuclearization is only on paper and disarmament does not work because treaties can be broken and often are. All nations can rearm with nuclear weapons because the secret atomic bomb recipe is out of the bottle.

It was—and still is—thought that the only way a nuclear war could be won would be by a first strike that precluded enemy retaliation. This was OK in 1945 when Japan did not have any atomic bombs, but today many nations have nuclear bombs that are far more powerful than the primitive ones used in 1945. They are so deadly that no one would survive a nuclear war.

The key-word here is "survive." Many do not realize

that only one or two modern atomic bombs are enough to kill everything around us. It does not matter who sends the first bomb: we will all be dead. There is no defense against ICBMs, with their minimal warning time.[145]

During the cold war between the Soviet Union and the United States, nuclear weapons were just what was needed to hold the superpowers back from war. Leaders of both countries were smart enough to not get involved in a suicidal conflict; I am unsure that was hold true of our leaders today.

If we want to live, we must solve the problems of climate change and pollution, and prevent the use of nuclear weapons. Even better would be an end to all wars. I know I am an idealist or naïve, but the billions and trillions of dollars spent on wars would be better spent on new technologies that help save us from disaster.

Nature has endowed us with a fantastic brain that permits us to as ask questions and solve problems. Yet, we seem unable to abandon the idea of war. Instead of helping each other and enjoying life, we kill ourselves for stupid reasons, such as religion, politics, and skin color. We have always invented better ways to kill one another, but today we have reached the point of no return.

The next global nuclear war will kill us all.

As I finish this book, it is August 7, 2019. I am an old man looking through one of the windows of my house that overlooks my quiet neighborhood. It is warm and I enjoy sitting in my garden enjoying the sight of blooming roses, my favorite flowers because they remind me of my youth and my parents' flower farm in Antibes on the French Riviera.

Life in this quiet neighborhood has been mostly the same

---

145 Russia announced that it has supersonic ICBMs that fly at 4 or 5 times the speed of sound.

for the last 40 years, except that people come and go. Children are born, grow up, and leave. People act the same. They use their cars as much as they did before they heard about climate change. They talk about the price of gas but not about decreasing the use of vehicles that pollute the environment. They live in a state—Michigan—where the car is king. Few people take the bus.

Except for a few storms, Michigan has been fortunate not to deal with types of weather that affect Louisiana, Florida, Texas. We are lucky to not have to fight wildfires like in California. Thus, it is hard for us to believe that the world as we know it is changing and worse, that it might disappear altogether.

But there are black clouds not in the sky, but on the political horizon. I just learned that President Trump thought of bombing Iran because the Iranians had shot down a U.S. military drone. But he changed his mind at the last moment. I cannot blame people for continuing with their lives. After all, if they were thinking about climate change and the threat of nuclear war all the time, they would not be able to function. But, if we do nothing, we are doomed. Are we going to continue to live in a world where we are threatened every day by the thought of a war that will destroy us all? Or a warming atmosphere that will make our planet unlivable? Shall we commit suicide?

Appendix 1

An atom is the smallest constituent unit of ordinary matter that has the properties of a chemical element. Every solid, liquid, gas, and plasma is composed of neutral or ionized atoms. Atoms are extremely small; typical sizes are around 100 picometers (one tenth-billion of a meter). They are so small that 100,000,100 of them set aside by side would be less than an inch long. But ever since that August day in 1945 when a mushroom cloud hovered above the devastated city of Hiroshima, the world has known what unbelievable power these minute entities possess.

Every atom is composed of a nucleus and one or more electrons bound to the nucleus. The nucleus is made of one or more protons and typically a similar number of neutrons. Protons and neutrons are called nucleons.

More than 99.94% of an atom's mass is the nucleus. The proton has a positive electric charge, the electrons have a negative electric charge, and the neutrons have no electric charge. If the number of protons and electrons are equal, that atom is electrically neutral. If an atom has a different amount of electrons than protons, then it has an overall negative (less) or positive charge (more), respectively and it is called an ion.

The electrons of an atom are attracted to the protons by

an electromagnetic force. The protons and neutrons in the nucleus are attracted to each other by a different force, the nuclear force, which is usually stronger than the electromagnetic force repelling the positively charged protons from one another. Under certain circumstances, the repelling electromagnetic force becomes stronger than the nuclear force, and nucleons can be ejected from the nucleus, leaving behind a different element: nuclear decay resulting in nuclear transmutation.

The number of protons in the nucleus defines to what chemical element that atom belongs: for example, all copper atoms contain 29 protons. The number of neutrons defines the isotope of the element. The number of electrons influences the magnetic properties of an atom. Atoms can attach to one or more other atoms by chemical bounds to form chemical compounds such as molecules. The ability of atoms to associate and dissociate is responsible for most of the physical changes observed in nature and is the subject of the discipline of chemistry.

Atoms are small enough that attempting to predict their behavior using classic physics—as if they were billiard balls—gives noticeably incorrect predictions due to quantum effects.[146] Through the development of physics, atomic models have incorporated *quantum* principles to better explain and predict what happens inside atoms.

The quantum world is seriously bizarre. It is a world where things can exist in two places at once and become inexplicably linked, no mater how far apart they are. In the

---

146 Quanta referred to the chunks of light. The word was suggested by Max Plank.

realm of atoms, electrons and particles of light, objects seem to change their behavior when they are being watched. [147]

For all its paradoxes, quantum mechanics is the most powerful and exacting scientific theory ever devised. The theory's predictions matched experiment with ridiculous precision. By revolutionizing our understanding of atomic structure, it transformed every facet of science, from biology to astrophysics. Without quantum theory, there would not be an electronics industry, no cell phones, no Google, not even television. But *philosophically,* until now physicists have been stymied over the question of why the microscopic and macroscopic worlds seem completely different to us: the problematic nature of quantum mechanics reigns over the first, whereas the second observes more logical "classical" rules. Where does one realm end and the others begin? For all the weirdness of quantum mechanics, most scientists are happy to leave it be. They carry on using the theory to operate their atom smashers and dark matter detectors [148] and rarely to stop and ponder what quantum mechanics says—or doesn't —about the fundamental nature of reality.[149]

When an atom splits into two parts, either through natural decay or because it has been bombarded by other subatomic particles known as neutrinos, it releases energy. This process is known as fission. It has great potential as a source of pow-

---

147   Without quantum physics, there would not be no matter, no light, no sun and most importantly, no iPhones.
148   Others continue to use our knowledge to build better and better atomic bombs.
149   Adam Becker. *What is Real? The Unfinished Request for the Meaning of Quantum Physics.* (New York: Basis Books, 2018) Brian Clegg. The Quantum Age (London: Icon Books, 2014).

er. Nuclear energy can also be released by fusion of two light elements (elements with low atomic numbers). The power that fuels the sun and the stars is nuclear fusion.

Inside the atom, electrons whiz around a positively charged nucleus, but in theory, these electrons would lose energy and ultimately spiral into the nucleus. The stability of matter would be impossible. It was proposed that electrons move around in discrete orbits and cannot exist between two orbits. If they jump between two orbits, they emit a lot of energy.

The cloud of electrons surrounding an atomic nucleus is bound to the nucleus by the electric attraction between the negatively charged electrons and the positively charged protons in the nucleus. But that same electric force also tries to rip the nucleus apart—like charges repel, and the closer together they are, the more they repel. A typical atomic nucleus is 100,000 times smaller than the surrounding electron cloud, which itself is a million times smaller than the width of a human hair. At such close quarters, the electrical repulsion between the protons in the nucleus, left unchecked, would send them flying off at nearly the speed of light. Instead atomic nuclei are held together by an even stronger force, unimaginatively dubbed the "strong nuclear force." The strong force binds together the protons and neutrons in atomic nuclear. Neutrons are electrically neutral—hence the name—but they feel the strong force, just like protons. They play a crucial role in the nuclear tug-of-war between electrical repulsion and strong force reaction, aiding the latter without affecting the former. While the strong force is not quite strong enough to keep two protons together by itself, adding a neutron to the mix increases the "stickiness" of the strong force without adding any electrical charge, creating a stable atomic nucleus of two protons and one neutron (helium -3)

The nuclear struggle between the sticky strong force and the repellent electrical force ultimately depends on the size of the nucleus. For small nuclei, the strong force wins out easily, and adding more protons and neutrons generally just makes it stronger. But the strong force can only act for very short distances, comparable to the size of a proton itself—anything much larger than a trillionth of a millimeter (a distance known as one fermi) is too much for it. After a certain point, the nucleus gets too big, the electric force starts to win the tug of war and the nuclei become weaker as more protons and neutrons are added. Specifically, that point is around nickel (28 protons and 34 neutrons) and iron (26 protons and 30-32 neutrons). Bigger nuclei than that are less stable, and beyond a certain size—namely lead, which has 82 protons and over 100 neutrons—there are no stable nuclei at all.

Uranium is far past that point. With 92 protons, it does not matter how many neutrons you add to uranium it will eventually decay. But there are two forms of uranium nuclei that will stick around for billions of years before they decay: uranium-235 and uranium-238. The numbers refer to the total number of protons and neutrons in the nuclei: U-235 has 143 neutrons and 92 protons, for a total of 235; U-238 has three more neutrons, which make it slightly heavier. But they are both uranium: the chemical identity of an atomic nucleus is determined solely by the number of protons that it has. Nuclei with the same number of protons are different isotopes of the same element. They differ in weight but not in their chemical properties.

The two isotopes of uranium have very different nuclear properties. Specifically, hitting a U-235 nucleus with a neutron leads the nucleus *to fission*: it splits into two smaller nuclei, releasing a fabulous quantity of energy, along with a few free-floating neutrons. With enough U-235, the neutrons left over from fission will hit more U-235 nuclei, which will split, releasing even more neutrons and starting a chain reaction. Left uncontrolled in 120 pounds—a small sphere of the dense metal, less than twenty centimeters across—a nuclear chain reaction would explode with the power of 15,000 tons of TNT, enough to instantly level a small city. Controlling the reaction by absorbing some of the excess of neutrons would allow you to power a small city for days on end with the same 120 pounds of U-235.

U-238 is a different story. Three extra neurons give it a little more stability, so hitting it with a neutron won't split it as easily. This makes it impossible to build a bomb out of U-238. To build an atomic bomb you would need to separate from the enormous bulk of 238- and since the isotopes are chemically identical, the only way to separate them is to take advantage of the fact that U-238 is 1.3 heavier than U-235. This guarantees that nuclear power would be phenomenally difficult to achieve, requiring enormous quantities of uranium and city-sized industrial diffusion and centrifuge facilities.[150]

---

150   The number of centrifuges played a role in the Iran treaty in 2017. But nobody explained to the public what the role of those centrifuges was.

Appendix 2

One of the personal benefits from writing this book is that I had to learn some atomic physics. Like many of us, who are not physicists, I had a hard time understanding the nature of light. How can it be a particle and a wave? How can we explain the weirdness of quantum physics? We do not see the strange effects of quantum physics in our daily life. Why not? May be quantum physics is only the physics of tiny things, and does not apply to large objects—perhaps there is a boundary somewhere, a border beyond which quantum physics does not work. In that case, where is the boundary, and how does it work? And if there is no boundary—if quantum physics applies to us just as much as it applies to atoms and subatomic particles—then why does quantum physics so flagrantly contradicts our experience of the world?

I got some answers when I read *The Quantum World: The Disturbing theory at the heart of reality*.[151]

Is there a size limit when objects stop behaving as waves?

According to the laws of quantum mechanics wave-par-

---

151   *The Quantum World* (London New Scientist. John Murray Learning 2017), p 40.

ticle duality and quantum super positions apply not only to the macroscopic (microscopic?) world of electrons and atoms but to macroscopic objects too.

The boundary between the quantum world and the 'classical 'everyday' one has been weakening for years. In 1999 Anton Zeilinger and colleagues at the University of Vienna demonstrated that bucykballs—molecules of 60 carbon atoms—act like waves when they pass through gratings. And in 2003 the same team performed the feat with tetraphenylporphyrin, a large molecule related to chlorophyll, which set a new record for the heaviest object to show wave-particle duality.

Quantum effects have also nudged into the realm of objects visible to the naked eye. In 2010 researchers made a 0.06, millimeter-long super cooled metal strip simultaneously vibrate and not vibrate, putting it into a quantum superposition. The record is currently held by a cloud of 10,000 rubidium ions. Is there any limit to how large an object can be and still show quantum effects? Nothing in quantum mechanics says that this limit exists, but the more atoms an object has, the more likely those atoms are to interact with each other and their environment, destroying fragile quantum effects.

Will this new knowledge lead to a better world or a worse one?

Selected Bibliography

Becker Adam. *What is real?* (New York; Basic Books, 2018).

Christianson, Gale. E. *Greenhouse: The 200-year Story of Global Warming* (New York: Walker and Company 1999).

Clegg, Brian. *The Quantum Age* (London: Icon Books, 2015).

Freedman, Lawrence. *The Future of War*. (New York: Public Affairs, 2017).

Freedman, Laurence. *The Price of Peace. Living with the Nuclear Dilemma.* (London: Fire thorn Press, 1986).

Gosh, Amitav. *The Great Derangement* (Chicago: The University of Chicago Press, 2016).

Hawking, Stephen. *A Brief History of Time* (New York: Bantam Books, 2017).

Hawking, Stephen. *The Theory of Everything* (Phoenix, New Millennium, Inc 2007).

Latiff, Robert. *Future War. Preparing for the New Global Battlefield* (New York: Borzoi Book, 2017).

Oreskes, Naomi and Erick Conway. *The Collapse of Western Civilization* (New York: Columbia University Press, 2014).

Rich, Nathaniel. *Losing Earth: A Recent History* (New York: Farrar, Strauss and Giroux, 2019).

Scranton, Roy. *We Are Doomed. Now What?* (New York, Solo Press, 2018).

Shell, Jonathan. *The Fate of the Earth and the Abolition* (Stanford CA, Stanford University Press, 2000).

Time. Special Climate Issue. September 23, 2019.

"Welcome to Climate Change." *MIT Technology Review.* May-June 2019.

Zinn, Howard. *On War* (New York, Seven Stories Press, 2011).

Zinn., Howard. *Zinn Speaks: Collected Speeches 1963-2009* (Chicago IL: Haymarket Books, 2012).

www.ingramcontent.com/pod-product-compliance
Lightning Source LLC
Chambersburg PA
CBHW020533290526
45786CB00002B/849